HUMAN RESOURCES DEVELOPMENT

✳

Human Resources Development

✳

EDWARD B. JAKUBAUSKAS

C. PHILLIP BAUMEL

Editors

✳

Iowa State University Press, Ames, Iowa

© 1967 The Iowa State University Press
Ames, Iowa, U.S.A. All rights reserved

Composed and printed by
The Iowa State University Press
Stock # 833

First edition, 1967

Library of Congress Catalog Card Number: 67–26062

✳

Preface

THE CHAPTERS IN THIS BOOK DEVELOPED OUT OF A CONFERENCE ON Human Resources Development, sponsored jointly by the Industrial Relations Center, the Cooperative Extension Service (both at Iowa State University), and the Iowa State Manpower Development Council.

This Conference was held at Iowa State University on October 13 and 14, 1966. More than 200 participants attended the various sessions. Represented were national, state, and regional manpower officials, college and university professors, extension staff members, high school teachers and guidance personnel, as well as interested citizens representing business groups and other private organizations.

The speakers and participants at this Conference represented a wide array of federal, state, and private organizations involved in a wide spectrum of manpower and human resource development programs.

The chapters were developed from the Conference proceedings and prepared by eminent authorities in their respective areas. Some of the authors are responsible for carrying out complex programs at the state or federal level; others are research scholars involved in evaluating these programs.

The essential purpose of the Conference was to bring together a variety of people—professionals involved in social science research and governmental policy implementation and private citizenry concerned with the general problem of human resource development.

From this involvement of speakers and participants, research and action personnel, public and private agencies, it is hoped that more meaningful human resource development programs can emerge for Iowa and the Midwest—so that the process of adjustment of workers into and out of the labor force can be facilitated in the years ahead at minimal social and economic cost.

While the large number of participants exceeded initial estimates, an even larger number was unable to attend the meetings and requested copies of the final proceedings. This book is intended to fulfill that mission but even more importantly to serve as a model for similar cooperative arrangements for local and regional program development in the future.

Planning and organization of the Conference involved numerous people. The primary burden of planning the program, inviting speakers, and structuring the various sessions was carried out by James A. Socknat of the Iowa State Manpower Development Council and C. Phillip Baumel of the Department of Economics and the Cooperative Extension Service at Iowa State University. Also involved in the planning of the Conference were Ronald Powers, George Beal, Wallace Ogg, Lee Kolmer, and Virgil Lagomarcino—all of Iowa State University.

A pre-Conference publication, which included articles prepared for the Conference, was prepared and edited as a Special Issue of the *Iowa Business Digest* by Lewis Wagner, Larry Sgontz, and Edith Ennis—all of the staff of the Bureau of Business and Economic Research of the University of Iowa, Iowa City.

Recognition is also given here to the U.S. Department of Labor's Office of Manpower Policy, Evaluation, and Research which assisted in financing this Conference through the Iowa State Manpower Development Council.

The proceedings of the Conference were compiled and edited jointly by Edward B. Jakubauskas and C. Phillip Baumel of the Department of Economics, Iowa State University.

It is hoped that this volume will serve as a means for the dissemination of ideas and the promotion of new programs in the complex field of human resource development.

✸

Table of Contents

✸

Summary and Overview

✸

EDWARD B. JAKUBAUSKAS *and* **C. PHILLIP BAUMEL**

IN ESSENCE THE WEALTH OF A NATION, REGION, OR COMMUNITY IS based upon its ability to conserve, develop, and utilize its human resources. The recognition of the importance of this fact is not new. On the eve of the Industrial Revolution in 1776, Adam Smith, reputed to be the "founder of economic science," argued that the quality and quantity of manpower resources constitute the wealth of nations and entitled his great classic in that way. More recently writers such as T. W. Schultz have characterized human resources as a form of capital—a produced means of production and the product of investment.

Numerous writers have stated that our rate of economic progress depends heavily on the quality and quantity of available skilled manpower at all levels. Manpower is the basic resource. It is the indispensable means of converting other resources to mankind's use and benefit. It takes skilled manpower to discover and exploit natural resources, to mobilize capital, to develop technology, to produce goods, and to carry on trade. If a country is unable to develop its human resources it cannot build anything else.

Human resources development includes programs and processes by which the quantity and quality of skills and knowledge are increased. Included are elementary through higher education, vocational training, on-the-job training, as well as the whole gamut of health, rehabilitation, and welfare programs. All of these affect the ability of an individual to develop his innate capacities as a worker and as an effective citizen in his community.

As pointed out by James Socknat, manpower development is differentiated from the concept of human resource development. This change is more than an exercise in semantics. Manpower policy is limited to the direct labor market activities of the labor force. In contrast, human resource development includes a broader spectrum of activity (which includes manpower development) but encompasses also the preparation of people for eventual labor market activity through education, the elimination of pretraining and preplacement problems emanating from barriers which stem from individual inadequacy, social and institutional problems within society, and geographic and spatial obstacles.

The focus of this book is the recognition that the concern for human resources development stems from the complex array of diverse sources. Technological change creates a demand for new skills and makes other skills obsolete. Different rates of growth of regions and industries create a need for mobility of workers. Continued lack of opportunity among minority peoples indicates a need not only for skill development but for equal attention to the solution of social and psychological problems which precede the acquisition of skills and jobs.

In terms of regional orientation, the chapters in this book are concerned not only with national trends but with problems of Iowa and neighboring states. Within the general problem of human resource development in the nation as a whole, some chapters are concerned with the structural dislocation of manpower in rural-agricultural areas and the industrialization of former farm regions of the country.

The authors note the complex nature of the problems generated by human resource development—stemming from a wide array of sources. The role of technological change is noted in all of its complex ramifications, affecting both the creation and the destruction of jobs. Not only technology but also barriers to change arising out of numerous other factors are discussed.

CONCEPT AND PROBLEM OF HUMAN RESOURCES DEVELOPMENT

Is Human Resource Development a New Concept?

Harold Sheppard points out that the notion of human resource development is not new in our country. Current federal programs have been preceded by significant developments in the establishment of the public school system, the Northwest Ordinance which set aside tracts of land for schools, the Morrill Act which created our system of land-grant colleges, the GI bill of the 1940's, and the National Defense Education Act of the late 1950's. These are but a few of the many programs which indicate that the concern for the development of our human resources is not new but merely a continuation of past trends.

Earl Williams and Austin Miller agree with this contention, but all three authors seem to agree that newness does arise in terms of:

1. The existence of a more conscious and deliberate attempt to formulate human resource development policies in their own right rather than as a by-product of other programs and goals;
2. The social justice aspects of the program—a concern for the individual's needs, rights, and opportunities;
3. The importance of human resource development for economic growth and the "capital investment" nature of human resources.

The Role of Education

All the authors recognize the importance of education as a first step toward effective programs of human resource development. But significantly additional factors are deemed to be crucial. Williams and Sheppard emphasize consideration of socio-psychological factors. The contributing aspects of the role of the family in determining the values, attitudes, motivation, and general development of the individual are dramatically presented by Sheppard in citing the Moynihan and the Coleman reports. The essence of these reports appears to be that education is most effective if it is followed by changes in the behavior of the individual—basically by altering the complex family environment of the individual. Sheppard points out the need for further research in this complex area.

Williams continues the thesis of socio-psychological dimensions of human resource development and suggests that problems of dealing with the hard-core unemployed must be approached through a number of facets—utilizing a team of several specialists to cope adequately with an individual's problems.

Aggregate Demand vs. Structural Transformation

In past debates that have raged among economists on the relative merits of dealing with the problems of unemployment through fiscal and monetary measures vs. training and education, Williams takes a strong stand in favor of particularized measures dealing with the individual and his problems. He objects to massive and aggregative policies in dealing with problems that he considers best dealt with on a custom individualized basis. Sheppard and Miller appear to think along the same line.

Equal Opportunity

These three authors consider equal opportunity to be of greatest importance in programs for human resource development. Williams recognizes explicitly the great losses incurred to the community because of racial discrimination. Sheppard delves further into the factors of motivation, attitudes, and family relationship which are all inextricably related to discrimination and its effects.

Relationship of Human Resource Development to Other Aspects of Society

It is interesting that none of the authors discusses human resource development without reference to a broader framework. Sheppard and Williams mention the economic returns to human resource development and consider the analogy to capital and investment. All three go beyond the economic returns, however, and consider or imply the underlying nature of democratic society—social justice (Miller), equal opportunities for Negroes (Williams and Sheppard). Although economic growth is assumed to be an important factor—and human resource development an important aspect of this—these writers place a higher value upon the economic and social welfare of the particular individual.

Do We Need New Programs?

It is interesting to note that in regard to new programs, the authors seem to recommend the assimilation and refinement of existing programs rather than venturing into new areas. Sheppard particularly feels that pouring additional funds into "bricks and mortar" in education (or additional training programs) will yield fewer social benefits at the margin than additional investment in socio-psychological factors relating to the family, motivation, and attitudinal behavior. We seem to have reached a gestation period in which old programs must be evaluated, reformulated, and coordinated. There appears to be no pressing need for new programs on any large scale.

NEED AND DEMAND FOR HUMAN RESOURCES DEVELOPMENT

Given the importance of developing our human resources, what are the main factors affecting the composition of employment and industrial manpower requirements?

The General Framework

Boulding considers human resource development as a special case of general development. Knowledge is viewed as the driving force for the development of society as well as human resources—a form of capital stock in society.

Knowledge is developed through the learning process which itself is evolutionary and takes place as a process of selection or mutation. Human learning and the process of evolution—mutation—are similar and the source of both human resource development and the development of society.

Boulding's thesis is that all development, whether economic or human, can be explained in terms of an ecology or environment in which a selection process alters commodities, ideas, and knowledge.

The mutation process goes on in terms of the human capacity for learning. Impediments to learning affect the growth of society and consequently the development of human resources. Boulding's analysis indicates that all human knowledge exists in the mind and that a transformation occurs in which human knowledge is lost every generation. The key to development is the transmission of knowledge from one generation to another.

It is interesting to note that both Sheppard and Boulding cite the family as important to human resource development. Sheppard cites a specific study in which the attitudes and motivations of individuals—and consequent behavior and adaptability in the labor market—were affected by behavioral patterns in the family unit. Boulding's thesis is more general and indicates that at times family ties can act as a bind to human resources or societal development. Boulding also presents an interesting concept of "obsolescence or depreciation of knowledge." The more knowledge we gain, the more must be cast off in future generations as obsolete, useless, and often an impediment to development.

In regard to employment opportunities Boulding suggests that the paradox of an innovating, developing, and efficient industry is that employment opportunities tend to decline. Less efficient industries seem to experience stable and even growing employment opportunities.

In order to have favorable conditions for development, a society must experience a period of time in which it has favorable terms of trade. The same analogy applies to an individual. Full development of the individual's capacities can occur if he has a period of time in which he has "favorable terms of trade." If not provided by a wealthy or resourceful family, some other source is required. (Perhaps the GI bill, Northwest Ordinance, and the legislation of the 89th Congress provided more favorable terms of trade to some of the disadvantaged elements in our society.)

Boulding concludes with the interesting point that society and individuals must undergo the process of decision-making under conditions of uncertainty. In the face of greater demands for specialization there must remain a strong element of adaptability. How to achieve adaptability with specialization is the crux of the drama of human resources development.

The Impact of Change on Iowa and the Nation

The chapters by Weinberg, Eldridge, and Futrell are concerned with the specifics of change in Iowa and the country as a whole. Weinberg indicates that the manpower effects of automation have been much publicized in the press but that employment as a whole (and particularly in the service sector) has continued to grow rapidly. Boulding's contention that employment grows in less efficient industries appears to be close to Weinberg's analysis of service sector employment growth.

Weinberg points out that employment in the service sector of the economy was 50 percent of total employment in 1956. This increased to 60 percent in 1966, and by 1975 two out of three workers will be employed in the service sector. The rise in service employment appears to be heavily concentrated in the areas of education, health, and nonfederal governmental employment.

Weinberg concludes with a twofold plea for:

1. Greater employment opportunities for Negroes faced with the effects of technological displacement and the prospect of competing for less skilled jobs,
2. Avoiding the concept of using people to meet industry needs rather than the other way around.

Eldridge and Futrell give the picture as it affects Iowa and other states heavily oriented toward agriculture and agriculture-related industries. Eldridge indicates that, unlike most other industries, farm employment appears to be inversely related to farm output. Capital is replacing labor-intensive methods at a rapid pace—in fact, the next ten years will see an accelerated pace in farm consolidations. Current trends show clearly that farm size will expand, capital per farm will increase, and labor per farm will decrease. The transformation of the labor force in Iowa will be quite dramatic in the years ahead. Thousands of young workers will have to migrate from rural areas and seek employment in urban nonfarm jobs—possibly outside Iowa.

Gene Futrell's analysis supplements and expands the material presented by Eldridge. Manufacturing employment has been increasing in Iowa, particularly for durable goods manufacturing. Of greatest significance to Iowa has been the trend for greater employment opportunities for women in manufacturing. Since Iowa is and will continue to be heavily dominated by agriculture, it is not surprising that food and related industries offer the largest volume of job opportunities at present and will continue to do so in the future.

The implications of the Eldridge-Futrell thesis are clear. Iowa can expect to experience further population and labor force changes, possibly of a dramatic nature, in the next decade. Some of the displaced manpower will be absorbed in manufacturing, but many workers will be forced to leave the state because of "opportunity displacement." The impact will be hardest on the very young and the very old in rural farm areas.

Colmen's presentation underscores the preceding chapters. Boulding's concept of the obsolescence of knowledge is restated independently by Colmen. Much learning is and should be forgotten as knowledge changes over time. Training and retraining are to be a permanent part of one's work life in the future. Suggestions have been made that workers receive a year's sabbatical at the age of 35—with benefits to be paid out of Social Security funds. Less ambitious proposals call for continuous or periodic retraining programs for all workers in the labor force. The European experience of retraining for 1 percent of the labor force at all times is cited as a possibility for the U.S. economy.

The crux of Colmen's chapter is that the current manpower picture in the nation finds shortages existing side by side with unemployed human resources. What is the solution to this paradox? More economic growth can help, but the real solution is a recognition of the social benefits of education and training and the unequal burdens experienced by the disadvantaged and handicapped in the labor force.

Education and training must be preceded by the removal of barriers related to health, discrimination, illiteracy, etc. The social and human costs of *not* developing meaningful programs is staggering. These costs can ultimately be diminished by focusing upon an individual's adaptability to change in society. This can be achieved—after barriers are eliminated and education and training are brought to bear upon the problem—by emphasizing career development for everyone in the labor force as opposed to merely job placement.

BARRIERS TO HUMAN RESOURCE DEVELOPMENT

Before workers can be educated, trained, placed in jobs, or promoted to higher levels of responsibility, various barriers to development must be removed. The concern of these chapters is not only the why and wherefore of how people get training and education and find jobs but the broader problem of why some are denied or do not avail themselves of the opportunity to develop to their fullest capacities.

Kovarsky provides a broad framework for barriers of racial discrimination. Although the title of his chapter relates to "racial barriers and apprentice training," Kovarsky accomplishes much more than this.

Starting with the World War I period, Kovarsky traces the migration patterns of Negroes from the South to the North, from rural to urban areas, and from agricultural to manufacturing jobs. The major forces affecting the status and aspiration level of the Negro appear to be technological change which displaced hordes of agricultural workers from their traditional jobs, the abnormal demands during both world wars for workers of all skill levels, and the social changes in the post-World War II period which saw a sharp rise in the demand by Negroes for a higher aspiration level.

Not all factors have worked to the advantage of the Negro, however. While early white immigrants in the United States were able to achieve a favorable status by entering the ranks of skilled, blue-collar workers, this avenue is less desirable for Negroes since the greatest gains of employment are being made in professional and technical areas. Also, while World War II assisted Negroes in obtaining access to training, the depression of the 1930's closed off opportunities for virtually a whole generation of Negroes who were unable to take advantage of the great labor demand of the 1940's because of a lack of skill.

The most potent and overriding factor which has blunted the opportunity of Negroes has been the pure and direct problem of racial discrimination. To those who feel that the Negro has made progress, albeit slow progress, Kovarsky cites the high and unyielding ratio of Negro to white unemployment in the country (and in Iowa).

The picture on human resources develoment barriers due to racial discrimination is a pessimistic one. Kovarsky feels that changes will be slow and grudging. At the same time we can expect that Negro dissatisfaction will continue. Discrimination in the crafts is particularly serious and in most cases has been hardened through the use of hiring halls, discriminatory use of tests, and family preference relationships in hiring.

Technological change finds competition emerging between white females and Negro males for manufacturing and service jobs, with the latter in a decidedly inferior competitive position in the years ahead.

Physical and Mental Barriers

Harrington's discussion relates to physical and mental barriers to human resources development. He objects to the viewpoint of redesigning people to fit jobs or of thinking in terms of filling industry's manpower needs. Calling for acceptance of "people as they are," Harrington argues that the greatest revolution has taken place not in the hardware of technology but rather in a change of attitude on the part of people toward the physically and mentally handicapped. Great progress has been made as a result of this changing attitude.

A final caveat suggested by Harrington: We should exercise care in accepting people for what they are rather than change them simply to fit the mold of our preconceived notions of what they ought to be or ought to do.

Institutional Barriers

James Thomas discusses barriers emanating from institutional factors. His discussion is concerned with institutional barriers in regard to law, custom, and demographic patterns. Attitudes of people in following the letter of the law only within certain limits and ignoring the spirit of legislation are criticized. Also, the case-by-case approach appears to Thomas to be a tedious, high-cost, low-effectiveness approach in dealing with the barriers of discrimination.

Spatial and Geographical Barriers

Ronald Powers mentions some of the barriers to human resources development arising out of spatial and geographical sources. He believes that great benefits could be attained through more investment of time, effort, and research into an understanding of how our social and economic system operates. Powers' thesis is that there seems to be an unwarranted fear of planning in our system of values which operates as an obstacle to meaningful solutions to community problems. Much could be accomplished in solving many of our human resource problems if people could avoid the extreme bias and fear of planning.

Powers also recommends better knowledge of labor market processes, particularly in relation to how people learn about occupations and how they develop careers. He opposes concentration of all manpower (human resource) services in one central city. The economies of scale of various services are such that the relevant geography surrounding a central city would vary from one program to another.

Powers further suggests that more attention be given to the problems emerging from the increased amounts of leisure time that will be experienced by all segments of the population in the future.

NEEDED DIRECTIONS FOR HUMAN RESOURCES DEVELOPMENT

Sylvia McCollum points out the great need for vocational education by citing the fact that 8 out of 10 students now in elementary school will not graduate from college. During the 1960's alone, 21 million noncollege graduates will enter the labor market and in addition, 3 million more wives, mothers, and widows as well as millions more who will be in need of additional job-related education. Are vocational education programs prepared to meet this need? Sylvia McCollum paints a bleak picture of the state of vocational education prior to 1963—and in some cases even today. Vocational education programs have been limited both in subject matter coverage and in geographical availability to those in need. Often courses have not been geared for emerging occupational fields.

While Colmen and Sylvia McCollum both term the situation in vocational education a "crisis," it appears that at least in this area the federal government has not failed to act. The federal government's investment in vocational education escalated from some $60 million in 1963–64 to $177 million in 1965–66. For 1966–67 the appropriation is scheduled to go up to $225 million.

Sylvia McCollum cites many areas of progress of the federal government in developing more effective programs for the years ahead. It is interesting to note that action is called for to broaden vocational education, to include preparation for life for an individual as a distinct human being rather than a more narrow concept of a labor input into an industrial machine. She believes that general education must be strengthened as the basic foundation for an effective system of vocational education.

If vocational education for the noncollege bound represents a massive problem for the country, education for the college bound represents a selective quality problem. Again Koenker offers the caveat that much more must be considered in human resources development in this area than just "physical inputs."

The problems facing colleges and universities in meeting the needs for human resources development in this area are related basically to the large bulge in population in the age group 14–25 in the 1960's. Add to this the growing demand for professional and technical personnel in the labor force and the pressure on higher education planning is indeed impressive.

From the qualitative viewpoint Koenker calls for better methods for identifying talented students in high school who have a potential for effective college work. While a majority of the gifted do find their way in higher education, a sizable number of those who have college ability are lost in the process through a lack of opportunity and/or motivation.

Koenker notes the wide disparity of burden of higher education among the states. In many cases high burdens (dollars for higher education per $1,000 personal income) are correlated with the export of talent to other states. Federal aid to higher education seems to find its most effective argument on this point.

The conventional wisdom regarding the projected large-scale future shortages of college teachers finds little support from Koenker. Citing a study by Allan Cartter, Koenker feels that demand and supply will be in balance about 1980.

Somers' provocative discussion serves as a warning to those who may be overly complacent with the success of current human resource-manpower programs. As one who is sympathetic to the need for human resource development, Somers, nevertheless, raises serious questions in regard to present programs.

First of all, from the conceptual point of view Somers rightly feels that a differentiation of definition is needed. There is a difference between: (1) the development of human beings, (2) human resources development, and (3) manpower development. Somers is concerned with a more limited concept of manpower development, the human factor in production, and within this area he evaluates two federal programs—the retraining program and the labor mobility demonstration program.

Among the questions raised by Somers regarding the programs are:

1. Are MDTA programs really effective in removing people from the ranks of the unemployed—over and above what the situa-

tion would have been without retraining?

2. Assuming that training programs are effective, how do we know where occupational training would yield the most favorable cost/benefit ratio?

3. Would it be more effective to expand employer OJT programs rather than to put money into institutional classroom programs?

4. Would an expanded labor mobility assistance program be more effective in raising employability than training?

5. If mobility programs are expanded, would these contribute to the structural imbalances in areas losing workers and create further problems?

6. Would movement of workers in labor mobility programs further accentuate employer patterns of discrimination against minority group workers and others?

7. In regard to more general questions, how do we know that one program is better—more effective per unit cost—than another?

Somers seems to feel that the period of program experimentation from 1961 to 1966 is rapidly coming to an end. Congress will be much more selective in funding programs and will want to know the relative benefits of the various programs. Selectivity will be the keynote of future Congressional action in human resource-manpower programs.

Summary

It is difficult indeed to summarize the many separate strands of thought presented by these chapters. There are differences in relation to content and emphasis and possibly some areas of disagreement. For the most part the various writers would agree that:

1. A high level of economic activity is a prerequisite to full development and utilization of human resources. Training programs and programs to remove barriers of discrimination can be effective only if the general level of economic activity is high.

2. The concept of human resources development must include more than training and education. The totality of the individual's problems—as complex as they might be—must be considered in discussing preparation for activity within and withdrawal from the world of work.

3. A good system of general education must precede vocational education. In fact, general education seems to emerge as the backbone of human resources development.

4. However, in dealing with the problems of the disadvantaged

and the handicapped and the hard-core unemployed and underemployed, one must go beyond questions of education and investigate problems of behavior conditioned by family and community environment.

5. Vocational education programs must be subject to close scrutiny to be sure that training is relevant to emerging occupational employment needs. Yet the welfare of the individual worker must be considered above the needs of industry. Workers are not to be considered as mere inputs into an impersonal economic production process.

6. Basically, no new federal programs appear to be needed. An evaluation of existing programs seems to be in order, however.

7. Barriers to full utilization and development of human resources will not be eliminated solely by economic growth and prosperity. Effective legislation is needed as well as effective enforcement of legislation.

8. The aggregative effects of automation have not been a problem in causing either unemployment or underemployment. However, the particular effects on certain industries—farming and agriculture—or the impact upon certain groups—Negroes, farmers, youth—can be significant.

9. Economic and educational opportunities must be increased for all groups; yet we must be able to identify the highly talented and motivate them to develop to their highest potential.

10. Locally, Iowa can anticipate further population declines and labor force dislocation as technology and farm consolidations accelerate the pace of change in rural farm areas. Some employment increases are anticipated in manufacturing but not enough to stem the outmigration of people from the state.

HUMAN RESOURCES DEVELOPMENT

CHAPTER 1

✹

✳

Theory and Concepts
of an Active Human Resources Policy*

✳

JAMES A. SOCKNAT

IN THE 1964 MANPOWER REPORT OF THE PRESIDENT TO CONGRESS, President Johnson announced an active manpower program as a specific instrument of national policy. This announcement was not a startling one. The 1963 Manpower Report of the President contained a discussion of the "emergence" of a national manpower policy as can only be prepared by a hopeful bureaucracy when an announcement of national policy provides firmer ground for the annual trek to Capitol Hill to appeal for authorizations and appropriations. Whatever part the vested interests of the bureaucracy played, however, the threads of the emergence of the policy can be traced back a considerable length of time.

The Northwest Ordinance provisions for free education, the Morrill Act establishing the land-grant colleges, the Smith-Hughes and George-Barden vocational education acts, the Wagner-Peyser Act establishing the federal-state Employment Service system, the

---

* Reprinted from the *Iowa Business Digest's* special issue on human resources development, October, 1966, University of Iowa, Iowa City, Iowa.

JAMES A. SOCKNAT is Deputy Director of the Iowa State Manpower Development Council, Des Moines, Iowa.

Employment Act of 1946 setting forth full employment as a national policy, and the employment programs of the Kennedy Administration—Area Redevelopment, Manpower Development and Training, and Trade Expansion—had all led up to the presence of a sufficient arsenal of weapons to attack problems of the labor force so that a national policy was deemed necessary to provide cohesion and a theoretical framework in which to deploy these weapons in an orderly fashion.

It is suggested herein that national policy go one step beyond an active "manpower" policy to an active "human resources" policy. This change would represent more than an exercise in semantics. The crux of the difference is in the limitation of manpower policy to labor market activity of the population,[1] whereas an active human resources policy would recognize the intrinsic value of human resources and would systematize the programs of human resources conservation, development, and utilization for ends beyond insuring an orderly demand-supply equilibrium at full employment. An *active* policy connotes a positive, responsible role of the government in policy, planning, and programming. Since inaction as well as action has its price, both in economic and social consequences, an active policy involves the weighing of consequences of inaction vs. action as well as of various action alternatives. The suggested shift from "manpower" to "human resources" implies no change in the active nature of the policy.

Before exploring the reasons for the shift to, and the ends of, an active human resources policy, it may be well to define each of the three components of the policy and to briefly explore some current and proposed programs as they would fit in the overall conceptual structure.

HUMAN RESOURCES CONSERVATION

As with land or capital, certain positive steps must be taken to maintain or conserve the human resource. Current programs falling within the scope of human resource conservation include workmen's compensation, unemployment insurance, welfare categorical relief programs, and the like which are designed to afford the indi-

---

[1] Verification of this statement is found in the *1964 Manpower Report of the President*, page XIII, wherein "the three fundamental goals" of the active manpower policy are set out as follows:
  "The first is to develop the *abilities of our people*.
  Another is to create *jobs* to make the most of those abilities.
  The third is to link the first two, to *match people and jobs.*"
  (Emphasis in original)

vidual a subsistence or minimum standard of existence. Into this same category fall minimum wage legislation, Social Security, Medicare, and mental health programs.

The distinction between conservation and development may be illustrated by reference to a program of the New Deal era. The Civilian Conservation Corps (CCC) was essentially a human resources conservation measure. This program created jobs for people, but the program was really not designed to develop skills. Few of the corpsmen were even expected to make careers in recreational areas development and land conservation. To the extent that the CCC worker gained skills or work habits, this program could be classified as a human resource development program. But such skills and work habits as the corpsmen developed were by-products rather than the central aim of the program.

The importance of distinction between conservation and development is especially critical in analyzing the need for or uses of a given human resource program. The proposed negative income tax currently advocated by some exponents of both the political left and right is a case in point.[2] Some have claimed the negative income tax to be *the* panacea which will eliminate the need for nearly all social welfare and antipoverty programs. Under the human resources policy categories conceptualized in this article, however, the scheme would clearly be a conservation measure. It does not in and of itself develop or utilize the human resource. It may assist the individual in breaking out of a poverty milieu, but only if the recipient expends, or more accurately invests, this government largess or rightful due, as you please, on such services as education, training (development), or transportation to a job (utilization). The point being stressed here is that the merits or demerits of any human resources program can be discussed more ra-

[2] The proposed program would work as follows: Congress would set a minimum annual income level, probably the current levels used by the poverty program. Each "taxpayer" would file a return. Those with incomes below the Congressionally established minimum would receive from the government a "negative tax" or payment based on the difference between his actual income and minimum. If the negative tax rate were 100 per cent, the "taxpayer" would receive the full difference between his actual income and the minimum. If the negative tax rate were 50 per cent, he would receive half the difference; e.g., assume an urban family of four:

Annual minimum income for urban family of four	= $3,000
Actual annual income for that family	= 2,000
Difference	$1,000

If negative tax rate is:
a) 100%, then 100% of $1,000 = $1,000 payment to "taxpayer"
b) 50%, then 50% of $1,000 = $ 500 payment to "taxpayer"

tionally if all concerned agree as to the purpose or purposes of the program. It is suggested that the three categories of conservation, development, and utilization provide a suitable frame of reference for program analysis.

HUMAN RESOURCES DEVELOPMENT

Human resources development programs are those processes by which the quantity and quality of skills and knowledge are increased. Elementary through higher education, vocational training, on-the-job training, and various habilitation programs are all development programs. Occupational mobility, too, is generally a process of development.

A development program is susceptible to examination from several points of view. For whose purpose is the development—the individual or society? For what ends is the development—employment per se, income satisfaction, or nonmonetary reward? Is the purpose immediate or long-run? And finally, what program or system is best able to meet the objectives?

Where one starts in asking the questions, or more correctly, how thoroughly one asks all the questions, will significantly affect the answers. To the extent that not all questions are asked, the matrix, as it were, of considerations is imperfect. The economist, for instance, will advise investment in development through education and training as long as the return, traditionally limited to measurement of income realization, exceeds the investment. Through cost-benefit analyses he can suggest which programs yield the best returns. But it may well be that a concern for social justice and individual dignity should permit or even encourage development to be pursued beyond the point of marginal economic return. Habilitation of the most severely retarded or continuation of education for the retiree might be activities for which the economist would find no marginal economic return but which might well be justified on noneconomic social bases. As more and more ends have become acceptable to build a Great Society, as determined through the political process, organized development programs have cropped up like "Topsy." It is at least worth considering a review and redefinition of development objectives and programs by a run through the development considerations matrix and the outlining of needs and demands (on whatever justification) and the pinpointing of gaps, duplication, and possibilities for program streamlining.

HUMAN RESOURCES UTILIZATION

Allocation of the human resource to permit its fullest use has been characterized in the past more by its absence than by its success. In part, no doubt, this is a function of our reluctance to acknowledge that the "invisible hand" portrayed by Adam Smith will not guide us into the most profitable expenditure of time and talent. But our collective actions have been in sharp contrast at times to a hallmark of a democratic society—maximum freedom of the individual. The prohibitions of discrimination of the Civil Rights Acts on the basis of sex, color, or national origin, and the "equal pay for equal work" amendments to the Fair Labor Standards Act[3] are just two examples of recent legislation to strike down artificial barriers to human resource utilization.

Problems of utilization, however, go beyond the need for destruction of artificial barriers. An adequate system of facilitating optimum utilization requires an adequate supply of counselors and guidance personnel and a smooth functioning mechanism for the compilation and distribution of information to match supply and demand, be that men and jobs, leisure and recreation facilities, or students and educational settings. For the labor market, the Employment Service has been the primary matching device. For a variety of reasons, the Employment Service has not been noted for success in meeting the needs of several categories of job seekers for information on employment opportunities. Likewise, all too many firms have been unwilling to post job vacancies with the Employment Service offices. The flood of human resources development programs in recent years has consistently called for counseling and guidance as an integral part of the programs. Yet the shortage of professional counselors goes on, with only token efforts to increase the supply of counselors to meet these new demands. And as the work life ends sooner and sooner through early retirement programs, including both Social Security and private and collectively bargained pension plans, there looms ahead another sizable demand for preretirement counseling.

A general absence of pension portability, lack of an adequate definition of underemployment, lack of job vacancy information, and the barriers to employment encountered by youth and older workers are all unsolved problems of human resources utilization.

---

[3] While equal pay for equal work does not per se increase utilization, the striking down of "women's" jobs and abolition of dual seniority systems under the amendments will increase human resources utilization by opening up new jobs for women.

And lest we pride ourselves on our phenomenal geographic mobility, which is surely a facilitator of human resource utilization, we need only remember such glaring unsolved problems as the Appalachia residents—unwilling to move out despite the absence of employment opportunities in the area, and the residents of megalopolis' inner city blight areas—unable to find their ways to service jobs available for the asking in outlying suburban districts.

THE SHIFT FROM MANPOWER TO HUMAN RESOURCES

To the human resources development consideration matrix suggested earlier should be added a similar set of questions for conservation and utilization. The resulting three-dimensional matrix would be the framework for production of an active human resources policy. Why shift from manpower to human resources? There appear to be three basic reasons: (1) individual dignity and social justice; (2) technological change, automation, and cybernation; and (3) program administration in a Great Society of creative federalism.

INDIVIDUAL DIGNITY AND SOCIAL JUSTICE

The necessity of each individual securing his place in society through work has traditionally been accepted as the modus operandi in our society. Philosophically, the notion has roots in Calvinistic theology. As the economy in the United States developed more or less along the lines of laissez faire capitalism, the notion of salvation through work was reinforced—at least to the point that the ordinary individual had no other alternative to work as a way of providing for himself and for his family.

Federal government manpower programs came when needs were recognized in the form of widely felt domestic economic demands or external threats to the nation. The needs of the country for food prompted assistance in the form of land-grant colleges and vocational agriculture training and education. A federal-state system of employment services came only after the experience of the 1930's. The international economic threat of the European Common Market was responsible for passage of the Trade Adjustment Act of 1961. The Act contained retraining provisions for those workers in the U.S. firms displaced because of the increased foreign competition which resulted from tariff cuts to be effected under the Act. The appearance of Russia's Sputnik caused the National Defense Education Act (NDEA) of 1958. NDEA got the federal government into the college education loan business, provided National Defense Fellowships, and rendered financial assistance to schools for strengthening science, mathematics, modern foreign languages, and related subjects deemed necessary for maintenance of the U.S. position of scientific primacy.

One can take this hypothesis one step further and argue that despite the moralistic overtones of statements made in announcements of programs providing for summer employment for youth and various projects designed to afford opportunities for minorities, the programs are really defense mechanisms to prevent disruptions and riots. Witness the flood of employment programs for youth going to the "hot spot" cities each summer to prevent "long hot summers." As any pragmatic state or local manpower program planner knows, a small Watts-type riot or disruption will bring the federal manpower money in faster and more easily than any amount of planning and designing for comprehensive human resource development and utilization.

To the above type of threat impetus, one must add the rationale of reward for past service. The most dramatic examples have been the GI bill and, more recently, the Cold War GI bill. It was not until the war in Viet Nam became unseasonably warm and affected the lives and families of a good many constituents that Congress finally passed the Cold War GI bill. This was true despite the cost-benefit studies showing that the cost of the original GI bill was returned to the federal government many times over through increased tax revenues.

To acccept the hypothesis that federal education and training programs were answers to specific national threats or were rewards for past service is not to vitiate the programs, but this hypothesis does strengthen the credibility of the converse conclusion—that is, that federal government manpower programs have not resulted from a basic belief that such programs are a sound social and, in most cases, economic investment in the human resources of this country. In short, it is at least open to doubt if a manpower policy's goal of supply-demand equilibrium at full employment really provides an appropriate opportunity for considerations of social justice. It might be worthwhile in a Great Society to hedge the issue enough to take into account enough ends to cover the individual who feels that "They also serve, who only stand and wait."[4]

TECHNOLOGICAL CHANGE, AUTOMATION, AND CYBERNATION

Whether one's conception of the economy of today is an economy with a rapid rate of technological change, as the age of auto-

---

[4] John Milton, "On His Blindness."

mation, or even as a cybernated society, the fact remains that the relative position of many individual workers in relation to land and capital in the goods and service-producing sectors of the economy is markedly different than in the days of earlier generations. And one need not look back too many years to find striking contrasts. Of course, there have been cries of fright over impending technological change dating back to Aesop's fables. And while the argument over the *rate* of change and its implications are and ought to be of interest and concern, it might be profitable to look to the reasons for society's attention to the problems of change.

If one looks to current reasons for the increased attention given to the phenomenon, it is tempting to assert that part of today's alarm is due to the fact that the technology of today threatens a different slice of the social structure than has been threatened for several centuries. That is, insofar as the highly skilled, the white-collar workers, and the professionals are adversely affected by technological change, the establishment is shaken. It may be a fair analysis to say that the economic establishment of a society has not been, or at least has not seen itself as being, so vitally affected since the demise of the feudal lords at the time of the industrial revolution. Part of this argument is based on the recognition of a considerably larger proportion of the population as belonging to the establishment by way of having achieved middle-class economic and social status. Thus, the number of those who worry about the loss of jobs has increased, and often quite correctly. The concern has been over unemployment which has resulted from:

1. Plant relocation (usually coupled with plant modernization as in textiles and meat packing),
2. Processes automation (as in longshoring and information storage and retrieval),
3. Product competition (for example, the container industry wars between plastics, metals, and glass), and
4. Cybernation (for example, engineering *design* by machine instead of by engineers).

At the same time that the "ins" have been put in the uneasy position of seeing machines compete for their jobs, they have seen the "outs" (the minority groups, the functionally illiterate, the disadvantaged, or whatever term is in vogue at the time) more vocal than ever before. And the "outs" have not been unaware of the need for occupational opportunities and income security. The civil rights organizations, the community action agencies sponsored by the Office of Economic Opportunity, and the private organizing done by activists such as Mr. Saul Alinsky, the unions, and others have all contributed to enabling the demands of the "outs" to be heard.

An example of such demands by the "outs" to get "in" at a time when external technological threat seems to exist is the demands by nonwhites for entrance into the building trades unions where a number of the locals are still lily white. The share of construction employment going to bricklayers, for instance, has been decreasing as product competition (e.g., precast concrete and steel) has increased. And the entry of minorities into occupations has historically come when the demand for the occupation has peaked and is on the downslope. The implications, of course, are that the minorities are in for continued frustration as they repeatedly "break through" into an occupation only to ride it downhill demand-wise. And the frustrations of the "outs" who have successfully broken "in" will be greater and greater as the life span of the downhill slope of the occupation decreases because of the increasingly rapid rate of technological change.

While the progress of technology produces a constant and individually agonizing reallocation of job opportunities among the labor force participants, some of the hardest questions yet to be answered center around the use of the greater amounts of leisure time resulting from the increased productivity of our economy. The trend of shorter hours in the work week has leveled off, and the increased leisure has come through more paid holidays, longer vacations, and a shorter work life through delayed entry into the work force and earlier retirement. If this trend is beyond control, or if it is controllable but is judged to be desirable, then the question that arises is whether there are adequate recreation and leisure facilities at which people can spend their holidays, vacations, and nonlabor force participation years. Further, are those who have the leisure educated to enjoy it, assuming adequate facilities? Or are they captives of an educational and social system which has perpetuated (or is it perpetrated?) the puritan ethic of work to the point where leisure is not regarded as having a dignified place in the social system? If leisure has no intrinsic dignity, building into society a system of education and development for leisure presents an enormous task.

Estimates of the macro effects of technological change, automation, and cybernation and the ability of our society to absorb and control them have varied from the essentially optimistic findings of the National Commission on Technology, Automation, and

Economic Progress[5] to the dire predictions of the Ad Hoc Committee on the Triple Revolution[6] or Donald Michael's *Cybernation: the Silent Conquest.*[7] Regardless of the point in the spectrum of projection with which one identifies, there is little doubt but that there will be serious micro disruptions as well as blessings in store because of these changes. How to reduce the disruptive effect to a minimum and to spread the benefits most appropriately would seem to require that the kinds of change, their rates, and their implications be rather comprehensively examined on a continuing basis to enable our society to alter its entire gambit of human resource programs, not just its manpower and economic policies.

PROGRAM ADMINISTRATION IN A GREAT SOCIETY OF CREATIVE FEDERALISM

As evidenced by the title of this subsection, bureaucrats seem to be born with an ability to pick up and incant cliches. Eventually the cliches take on meaning. The phrase "Great Society" at least raises a reaction in most people, if not a crystal clear vision of what it is. But since the phrase "creative federalism" has not yet been defined by its author,[8] it is assumed that it is still open season for giving it a meaning. On that assumption this article proceeds. The term creative federalism conjures visions of at least the following elements: (1) new approaches to meeting societal problems (thus creative); (2) sharing in innovation and decision-making by the states and Washington (thus federal); (3) use of federal tax revenue to finance part or all of the new approaches (since it was then CEA [Council of Economic Advisers] chairman Walter Heller's proposed tax rebate plan that gave impetus to reexamining federalism) in light of conditions in the latter half of the twentieth century; and (4) the Appalachia Commission (because the program has been labeled as an example of creative federalism by the author of the phrase).

---

[5] See the Commission's report, "Technology and the American Economy," Feb., 1966.

[6] The Ad Hoc Committee on the Triple Revolution in March 1964 sent a 29-page statement to President Johnson and members of Congress urging a drastic reorientation of distribution of the national product by such means as a Guaranteed Annual Income. The 32 signers of the statement based this need on the interrelated revolutions of: (1) cybernation, (2) modern weaponry, and (3) human rights demands taking place throughout the world, and evidenced in the United States by the civil rights movement.

[7] Santa Barbara Center for the Study of Democratic Institutions, 1962.

[8] President Johnson introduced this term in a May 22, 1964, Ann Arbor, Mich., speech; this was the same address in which he first outlined "The Great Society."

When one looks at the difficulty of planning and coordinating the numerous elements of a human resources policy in light of the myriad of federal programs available and agencies responsible, it is awesome. But to add to this the assorted structures of 50 state governments with personnel of varying degrees of competence within and among them, and with differing needs and preferences in each state, the task appears even more dismaying. However, the integration of the manpower, education, rehabilitation, health, and all the other component programs into an active human resources policy need not spring into existence full blown, nor need it reduce the states to the role of subservient lackeys of a domineering Washington bureaucracy. Each state might start by preparation of a Human Resources Report containing: (1) an atlas of human resources; (2) a roster of goals and priorities for human resources conservation, development, and utilization in light of the state's human resource atlas; (3) an inventory of existing human resources programs—federal, state, local, and private; (4) an assessment of the current programs listed in the inventory against the backdrop of identified human resource goals and priorities, thus bringing to focus the gaps, duplication, and possibilities for simplification and streamlining of human resource programs.

If the state were unable to prepare the Human Resources Report with its existing resources, it might apply for a planning grant (for example, Section 701—Urban Planning Assistance Program under the Housing Act of 1954 would seem to be appropriate).

To create leverage on the states to conduct human resources planning, the federal government might eventually require a comprehensive human resources plan application which would take the place of the numerous limited-purpose grant-in-aid applications submitted by the states now. At present, state plans are required for Vocational Rehabilitation, Manpower Development and Training, Title I Higher Education, Mental Retardation, Community Mental Health Facilities, and various other monies. It appears that a requirement for a comprehensive state health plan will be in effect soon. Initially, the required human resource plan might take the place of half a dozen currently required plans. Each year additional grants-in-aid and other programs could be incorporated. The benefits of using the state Human Resources Report as a basis for the comprehensive human resources plan application are obvious.

As inducement to the states, the monies for funding the comprehensive plan would be made available in gross. Few if any minima or maxima proportion restrictions for component parts of the plan would be imposed. This would allow the states maximum latitude in programming to meet their goals and priority demands. The comprehensive plans would be reviewed at the national level by an interagency panel composed of personnel who have demonstrated breadth of vision and thus could be expected to keep interagency rivalry from clouding consideration of the comprehensive plans.

Under the current grant-in-aid system, an alarmingly large number of target groups are quantified only by assumption that the national percentage holds true for the state population. Even worse, this method of computation is often the most important or even sole determining factor in the derivation of each state's money allocation. Departure from such mechanical assumptions would force the development of better census data systems in the states.

And finally, the comprehensive human resources plan would invite a gradual overcoming of provincialism of both state and federal agencies and personnel as they become more aware of other legitimate competing needs of human resources conservation, development, and utilization.

After the states and the federal government have developed a degree of sophistication in the use of comprehensive human resources planning, a portion of decision-making power reserved to the federal government quite possibly could be delegated to regional interstate compacts, such as the Appalachia Commission, providing at the same time that a harder look be taken at the regional nature of human resources problems and allowing for more extensive use of regional cooperation on mutual problems.

✳

CHAPTER 2

An Experiment in Manpower Coordination: The Iowa State Manpower Development Council*

✳

EDWARD B. JAKUBAUSKAS and DONALD E. MITCHELL

THE IOWA STATE MANPOWER DEVELOPMENT COUNCIL GREW OUT OF a need felt by Governor Harold E. Hughes for a state agency to coordinate work in Iowa on the flood of federal legislation dealing with manpower and related areas. In the spring of 1965, Governor Hughes signed a contract for $492,950 with Secretary of Labor W. Willard Wirtz for the establishment of the experimental and demonstration project now known as the Manpower Development Council. The contract has a finite life of eighteen months—from June 18, 1965, to December 18, 1966.

The Manpower Development Council (MDC) has five functions: coordination, technical assistance, information, liaison, and special projects. To execute these functions, the Council was or-

---

* Reprinted as it appeared under the title "The Iowa State Manpower Development Council" in the *Iowa Business Digest's* special issue on human resource development, Oct., 1966, University of Iowa, Iowa City, Iowa.

EDWARD B. JAKUBAUSKAS is Professor of Economics at Iowa State University, Ames, Iowa. He was formerly Director of the Iowa State Manpower Development Council. DONALD E. MITCHELL is Chief of the Higher Education Branch, Iowa State Manpower Development Council, Des Moines, Iowa.

ganized into six branches: Special Projects, Rural Manpower, Disadvantaged and Handicapped (institutionalized or socio-economically deprived), Vocational Education and Training, Higher Education, and Research. Each branch was organized to help coordinate on-going work of Iowa agencies and groups; to offer technical assistance where needed; to provide information on programs and legislation; and to offer the service of liaison between Washington and Iowa and between Des Moines and the 99 counties of Iowa.

The Council is a state agency operating directly from the Office of the Governor and concerning itself with human resource development on a broad scale—considering those persons with the most modest abilities and those with the highest level skill. Fruition of the human resource development work of the Council will be development of a State Human Resource Development Plan. This plan will be based upon the premise that the maximum development of each citizen's capabilities is a function of the willingness of society to allocate a growing portion of its resources to health, welfare, and educational programs.

VAST INCREASE IN FEDERAL PROGRAMS

The need for a state agency to assist state and local groups and agencies, public and private, becomes obvious after an examination of the rapid increase in federal programs.

The federal administrative budget for 1965 for health, labor, and welfare totaled $5.8 billion. In fiscal 1966 this grew to $8.3 billion, and estimates for 1967 virtually doubled since 1965 to $9.9 billion.[1] In addition to this, the education budget grew over the comparable period from $1.5 billion in 1965 to $2.3 billion in 1966 and is estimated at $2.8 billion for fiscal 1967.[2]

From another point of view, a United States Department of Labor inventory of federally assisted manpower development programs lists 34 laws which are relevant for job training alone.[3] Another inventory published by the Office of Economic Opportunity lists over 250 federal programs affecting low-income individuals and communities.[4] Whether one considers the growth of federal expenditures in this field or the number and variety of programs, the role of the federal government in health, welfare, education,

---

[1] President Johnson's budget message submitted to Congress for fiscal 1967.
[2] *Ibid.*
[3] "Inventory of Federally Assisted Manpower Development Programs," mimeographed staff paper, U.S. Department of Labor, Aug. 24, 1965.
[4] *Catalog of Federal Programs for Individual and Community Improvement,* Office of Economic Opportunity, Dec. 15, 1965.

and manpower is truly impressive.

With this growing role of the federal government in the manpower development field, there has been a concurrent realization that the effectiveness of these programs would be enhanced through more efficient coordination. Coordination, in turn, involves the elimination of duplicating programs, but more importantly, it implies linkages of two or more programs to better serve the citizenry of the country. To meet this goal of efficiency, numerous varieties of administrative organizations evolved. At the national level, interagency cooperation has emerged to a great extent in processing and developing various project proposals. Problems remain for implementing full coordination at the federal agency level, but initial progress has been made in a number of multi-agency sponsored projects already.

LOCAL, REGIONAL, AND STATE COORDINATION OF PROGRAMS

Though coordination at the federal agency level is important for full utilization of human resource development programs, complete coordination must, in the final analysis, be developed at the local community level. It is at this point that the various independent threads represented by federal legislation and the numerous agencies in Washington are actually brought to bear upon the individual and his multi-faceted needs.

With the enlarged extent of human resource development programs, a concept of regional coordination has developed. Foremost as an example of this is the Appalachian Regional Development Program, financed in heavy part by special legislation to assist this region, but also involving other federal programs as well. Regional development programs of this type have led to the coining of a new phrase in government circles—that of "creative federalism." By this is meant that a redirection of federal grants-in-aid will emerge which will lessen federal requirements and regulations as to how the money is spent and also will direct funds to states organized on a multi-state regional level. State and local governments will be given the opportunity to formulate their own programs—using federal funds—with the federal government acting only if local governments fail to act. It is contemplated that with "creative federalism" an effort will be made to work through new types of structures such as area-wide bodies and private and semipublic groups.[5]

[5] See: "The Challenge of Creative Federalism," by Senator Edmund S. Muskie, *Saturday Review*, June 25, 1966. Also: "On Creative Federalism: Johnson Suggests New Intergovernmental Relations," *Congressional Quarterly*, Apr. 22, 1966, p. 832.

CURRENT POLICY PROBLEMS IN HUMAN RESOURCE AND MANPOWER DEVELOPMENT

For the layman (and very often for the active practitioner) manpower development programs present a confused and conflicting picture. Professor Harbison of Princeton University has noted that a lively debate has ensued in the field, with various calls for action in coordinating manpower programs, though no one has really come forth with a workable plan for coordination because no one has been able to really identify the goals that we are attempting to attain.[6] As Professor Harbison points out, little thought has been given either to the framework of coordination, the strategy, or the locus of power and responsibility for program development.

It takes little sophistication to observe that there is no "policy" of manpower development as such. Like "Topsy," the nation has forged ahead on all programs almost simultaneously. Training programs under the Manpower Development Training Act (MDTA) are emphasized in dealing with the problems of unemployment—yet, in 1965 the number of trainees in the country numbered 100,000 in comparison with an average level of unemployment during the year of 3.4 million. (The number of persons experiencing unemployment will, of course, be much greater over the years.) Even if we compare the number trained with the hard-core unemployed (775,000), the role of MDTA is not very significant. When we consider the fact that MDTA programs have not been geared to deal with the hard-core unemployed, the impact of this program appears to be even less significant. While much of public attention is focused upon training programs in dealing with unemployment, most economists actually are convinced that fiscal and monetary policy is of overriding importance in affecting manpower utilization.

In actual practice, manpower policy provides for programs that often operate at cross-purposes to one another. We have programs designed to keep workers from leaving rural areas—we have programs to facilitate their movement out. We have a vast network of 1,900 employment offices throughout the country—yet only a small fraction of total job placements are made through public employment offices. We have legislation designed for the unskilled and the poor, as well as legislation for those embarking upon careers in professional and subprofessional occupations. There is legislation for the establishment of permanent, specialized voca-

---

[6] "Critical Issues in American Manpower Policy and Practice," by Frederick Harbison, *Proceedings of the Seventeenth Annual Meeting of the Industrial Relations Research Association*, Dec., 1965.

tional education centers, for the utilization of private facilities for
on-the-job training in industry, and for "ad hoc" institutional classroom retraining for the unemployed. We find programs for the
young, the old, the urban, the rural, as well as the skilled and unskilled.

In short, manpower programs have evolved as a collection of
special-purpose "tools" dealing with specific short-run problems,
rather than as a part of any general pattern or conscious design. In
fact, the development of our manpower resources has been merely
implicit within broader social and economic programs and goals.
There has certainly not emerged an overall system for planning,
either at the state, regional, or federal level, for manpower and human resource development in its own right.

Each federal agency has viewed itself as a "coordinator" in the
manpower field, and in some cases competition has been seen even
among bureaus within the same department. At the state and local
levels, the effect of federal neglect has resulted in chaos, confusion,
and often rightful hostility.

The Search for a "Coordinated" Human Resource Development Program

The growth of federal expenditures on education, manpower,
and welfare and the vast array of legislation, programs, and proliferation of agencies and organizations dealing with various aspects
of manpower development have sharpened the need for a structure
or framework of coordination for manpower development. The
need is apparent, but the actual structure remains unresolved as
does the nature of the decision-making process of manpower development as such. Even the questions raised have been confusing,
with various proponents calling for either an "active," a "cohesive,"
or a "comprehensive" policy in the field. Not all of these things are
identical—even if we were able to achieve a consensus as to which
agency should perform the coordinating and where the coordination should take place.

Increasingly, questions of defining the meaning of manpower
development (and coordination) have been evolving in discussions
of the feasibility of planning manpower development programs.
The concept of *a* plan, imposed upon the individual or community
would be unacceptable within our system of government or values
of society. What is suggested here is the concept of "planning"—a
process rather than an achieved goal; an activity which involves
the needs of people as individuals rather than the autocratically
imposed will of a single individual or group; a program developed

at the community and state levels rather than one emanating from the federal level.

As an experiment in designing a coordinated, active, and comprehensive manpower program at the state level, the Iowa State Manpower Development Council was established. Its purpose was to weave the separate programs found at the state and federal levels into a purposeful fabric which would maximize effectiveness in raising the employability of the individual, and in assisting him in arriving at decisions in the labor force through knowledge and with the immediate availability of all resources enacted into law.

FORMATION OF THE MANPOWER DEVELOPMENT COUNCIL

The immediate need for an agency at the state level—such as the Manpower Development Council—became apparent when a "weak Governor" system of government in Iowa was called on to deal with a vastly growing federal manpower program. Federal programs, developed to meet the serious problems encountered in local areas, were applied in virtually equal proportions to all 50 states, mainly for political reasons. The "mix" of programs emerging from the federal agency level and applied to Iowa appeared to lack the capability of spontaneously meeting the optimal mix for Iowa. In some cases, projects could be brought into the state without the approval of the Governor; in other cases, projects could be brought in over his veto. At best, the Governor's office did not have the capability of keeping up with, and on top of, the rapidly changing federal scene. Decentralized clusters of state agency authority—virtually autonomous of direction from the state's chief executive—were emerging.

The Manpower Development Council was formed to meet two separate needs: (1) At the state level an agency was clearly needed to advise the Governor of developments in manpower training and to lessen the adverse effects of a "weak Governor" system which made the Governor responsible to the people but gave him virtually no power to implement his decisions. (2) At the federal level there was much uneasiness developing at high policy-making levels regarding *not only* the effectiveness of federal programs but also the efficient application and coordination of these programs.

The Council was established under a contract between the Office of the Governor of Iowa and the Office of Manpower Policy, Evaluation, and Research of the United States Department of Labor. (The authority for this grant is Title I of the Manpower Development and Training Act of 1962, amended in 1963 and in 1965. This section of the Act provides for unique and innovative projects in dealing with problems of unemployment and under-employment. It has received enthusiastic and unanimous endorsement by both parties in Congress.)

LAUNCHING THE MANPOWER DEVELOPMENT COUNCIL

On July 15, 1965, the Governor appointed the director, and the most unique experiment not only in the manpower field but also in federal-state relations was launched.

The first three months of operation constituted a "tooling-up" period. Office space was acquired; staff recruited and trained; and a rationale or philosophy of operation emerged. By mid-October, 1965, the Manpower Development Council was in operation. But before this took place, numerous problems had to be resolved before the Manpower Development Council could fulfill its mission.

First of all, there were the housekeeping chores of finding about 3,000 square feet of office space for a staff of 23 persons. A budgetary system and procedure for keeping financial records had to be devised to satisfy both federal and state requirements. At times these requirements worked at cross-purposes to one another, and there was little precedent available to assist those involved in coping with this unique situation. For example, the contract called for a separate and special bank account, but this was contrary to state procedures. Leasing and use of office equipment presented other problems. Federal regulations required the use of surplus equipment; this is an excellent procedure for most contracts; but for this operation the Council could not obtain the quantity of desks, chairs, and tables required at the time needed.

Over and beyond the mundane tasks of finding space and equipment, the climate in mid-1965 toward manpower and federal programs was not entirely a friendly one. The state Office of Economic Opportunity (OEO) was formed only weeks before the formation of the Development Council, and the aggressive director of that agency had attracted much attention in the press in forming community action programs and in waging the war on poverty. Some of the hostility intended for the state OEO had been directed in correspondence to the Council and vice versa. To complicate matters even more, the state OEO director and the MDC director found many areas of overlap and duplication in their respective mandates. These were resolved very quickly, however, and a spirit of cooperation which has continued to the present time developed between the two organizations.

Staffing the Council became the major preoccupation of the director in the initial three months. A number of serious constraints appeared in this activity. First of all, staff could be hired only for a period of twelve to fifteen months. Also, staff salaries for senior personnel were $12,000 per year, with junior salaries up to a ceiling of $9,600. The time of year—July to September—was not the most ideal period for recruiting.

Given numerous constraints, a remarkably intelligent and imaginative staff was recruited from July to October. Although many persons were lacking in direct knowledge of the manpower field, they had a high level of intelligence and high-spirited enthusiasm for the task at hand. The senior people who were recruited represented the following disciplines: economics, agricultural extension, geography, law, occupational therapy, social work, and journalism. Virtually all had some graduate work beyond the bachelor's degree, and the average educational level of all staff—senior and junior—was 18 years. At the junior level were represented personnel administration, political science, theology, and education. Most of the personnel were Iowa residents; others who were non-Iowans were from the Midwest.

Since most had had little direct experience in manpower programs, an intensive training period was launched with daily seminar-type sessions on all federal statutes relating to manpower and on guidelines in preparing project proposals. Federal officials cooperated in establishing in Washington training sessions involving high-ranking federal agency officials. Therefore, by mid-November the Manpower Development Council was prepared for its task, and the varied programs leading toward state level coordination were launched.

Mission of the Iowa State Manpower Development Council

The mission of the Manpower Development Council was five fold: (1) coordination, (2) technical assistance, (3) liaison, (4) information, and (5) special projects.

These five functions are explained below:

Coordination

The Council is attempting to bring to bear all resources available in the community and state to increase the employability of workers in the labor force; in addition, it will bring various "threads"—represented by the numerous programs in existence—into a larger and more meaningful fabric. Linkages in programs are the methods by which coordination is to be established among separate programs and agencies. The end result of the Council's activity here is to maximize the effectiveness of the various individual programs in accomplishing the mission of making workers more employable. In brief, the purpose is to maximize output per dollar of input of federal and state resources.

Some examples of coordination include the linkages of programs in dealing with hard-core unemployment—basic education plus MDTA institutional training plus MDTA on-the-job training. Such coupled programs are now on the drawing boards.

Coordination is also contemplated in the development of a regional compact in this six-state region for a flexible on-the-job training arrangement whereby training programs could be developed on a cooperative basis. This is an experiment in the concept of "creative federalism" at the regional and community levels. On-the-job training (OJT) funds would be coupled with economic development programs, area vocational schools, and institutional training. Funds not utilized for OJT in certain communities could be readily shifted to other areas of greater need.

Other examples of coordination include interagency meetings to discuss health occupational training needs, a prevocational counseling center, survey research needs for Iowa, the initiation of training institutes for various state agencies, five projects for Upward Bound for Iowa colleges, and unique programs in the utilization of Neighborhood Youth Corps funds in assisting the mentally retarded. The basic goal in coordination has been simple: Get the most "mileage" from individual programs by combining these in meaningful linkages—this, in turn, is accomplished by bringing agencies together in planning and implementation of projects.

Technical Assistance

One of the major functions of the Manpower Development Council envisioned by those establishing this organization was the provision of technical assistance to public and private agencies in drafting, writing, and developing projects through to eventual funding. This was to be particularly designed to assist local communities and small organizations lacking the resources to cope with the complexities of federal guidelines.

The on-the-job contracts developed (or in the process of development) in five Iowa communities was the classic illustration of this function. The OJT contracts involved negotiation at both the regional and federal levels, with ever-changing guidelines, deadlines, and operational procedures. Local communities were in no position to develop projects on their own volition in this area without a considerable expenditure of time in self-education. However, a number of problems emerged in giving technical assistance to or-

ganizations and communities. There was a tendency (not in the
OJT area) for an organization to seek assistance and to permit the
Council to develop a project, receive funding, and then in the final
analysis to remain dependent upon the Council for on-going operational responsibility. This was not the original intent of the
Council. The Manpower Development Council began to insist
that organizations contribute something of their time, money, and
staff in cooperating in the designing and writing of projects.

Information Dissemination

Of possibly the greatest importance was the third function of
providing better information regarding manpower development
nationally and at the state level. To implement this task, an on-
going monitoring system was developed regarding project guidelines from various funding agencies, and even monitoring proposed legislation at the national level. It is anticipated that this
information will be disseminated in a Council newsletter in the
future. On a less formal basis, manpower information has been
given to agencies largely in relation to developments at the federal
level.

Liaison

Closely related to the information function has been the development of better liaison with federal agencies at the regional
or national level. This has been a type of "ways and means" function in which state agencies have requested assistance, not in drafting proposals but in following through and in cutting some of the
"red tape" that invariably seems to develop in federal-state relations. On a number of projects we have taken the initiative of inviting federal officials to discuss project proposals with persons at
Iowa State University. (Possibly the most dramatic example of liaison is the Upward Bound program for Iowa in which $592,000 was
brought in for five Iowa colleges; a health occupational training
project is another good example.)

Special Projects

One mandate given to the Director of the Council by the Governor was to identify gaps in programs and areas of need for manpower development in the state. The special projects branch was
instrumental in bringing in $700,000 worth of contracts for on-the-
job training and employment opportunities for about 1,200 to
1,500 hard-core unemployed. This also included a prime contract
for the Council itself for $266,000 which is being used as a demon-

stration project of a statewide coordinated OJT operation. The problem is to see how a state agency can use OJT in conjunction with other manpower programs and also how to lend assistance to the cluster of OJT projects in the state. Plans for 1967 include the possibility of designing a flexible OJT program for the six-state region. Funds would flow more flexibly under this new experiment of "creative federalism."

Other special projects included the development of a Peace Corps unit for Iowa, focused upon "service employment" of older citizens, and the development of an OEO Vocational Rehabilitation sponsored alcoholism treatment and control project.

STRUCTURE AND ORGANIZATION OF THE
MANPOWER DEVELOPMENT COUNCIL

The initial structure of the Council provided for five major branches. Later, the special projects branch was added as a special area in its own right. In addition to special projects, there are others: Research, Higher Education, Disadvantaged and Handicapped, Vocational Education and Training, and Rural Manpower. Each branch is headed by one senior manpower specialist (except the Disadvantaged and Handicapped project, which has two). Also, provision was made for the training of junior specialists in the manpower field, to be used either as senior people later in the Council's work, or with other manpower agencies in the future. Each of the specialists works with a cluster of agencies in his area, carrying out the functions of coordination, liaison, information, and technical assistance.

For contract renewal, beyond December, 1966, the plan is to streamline the Council into three operational divisions (Division of Health Systems Development; Division of Social Systems Development; and the Division of Training). These divisions have, respectively, the missions of solving and removing obstacles to employability of health and other physical and mental handicaps; removal of obstacles of poverty and discrimination; and lastly, the development of more efficient methods for training those participating in the labor force, or—in the case of those retiring from the labor force—more suitable means for withdrawing from the world of work with dignity and creativity. Certain staff functions are also planned: area development planning, research, information to news media and public affairs, and a part-time position for the internal housekeeping operations of finance, management, and personnel.

The major change in organization will be the replacement of the program for manpower intern training, and in its place the installation of a system for the greater use of outside consultants and part-time, short-term, and temporary personnel. These would be added according to the needs as they develop on specific projects. Another feature is the establishment of a citizens' and public agency advisory committee to help direct the work of the organization.

FROM PROJECT APPROACH TO HUMAN
RESOURCE DEVELOPMENT PLANNING

One method used in the training of staff was the project approach. Each staff member was encouraged to develop ideas. These ideas were discussed and, if found to have merit, were moved to the project stage. Individual responsibility was emphasized, and project development was considered to contribute to the training of each staff member, as well as having merit in its own right. Project work has been generated from the needs and requests of other state agencies.

Between October, 1965, and June, 1966, the Council staff generated work on 65 projects, covering varied areas of manpower and human resource development. As of this date, dollar value of the projects is $5,065,000—although dollar value is only one measure of activity and not necessarily the most meaningful. As of this date, $3,575,789 had been either approved or funded. (This does not include the Manpower Development Council's own budget of $442,950 or the renewal request of $367,000 for 1967.)

By mid-June of 1966, the Council shifted away from a "project" approach to one which might be characterized as "human resource development planning." The project approach was useful as a training device and had merit in locating funds for some of the ideas; however, it can become a drawback without a general goal or philosophy of action.

The period of mid-June to October of 1966 has been designated as a "planning period." Staff members once again participated in seminars and workshops to exchange ideas and thoughts on the previous months of project development. Experiences and insights were exchanged on the activities of the various branches of the Council. The staff decided to prepare a "Manpower and Economic Report to the Governor," which was published in September, 1966. This report is part of the Council's responsibility to report to the Governor the "state of the State."

The Council plans to use knowledge of Iowa's trends as a guideline as to: (1) what Iowa will look like in the future (1980) if past trends continue; and (2) how the Manpower Development

Council can implement a program for maximizing Iowa's capability in achieving the goals determined by the needs and wants of the citizens of this state.

The keynote for planning the programs for 1967 and beyond was the Regional Conference on Human Resource Development held at Iowa State University in Ames, October 13 and 14, 1966. The conference was sponsored by three organizations: University Extension, the Iowa State University Industrial Relations Center, and the Manpower Development Council. We believe that this conference has set the theme for continuing regional human resource development.

IDENTIFICATION OF PROBLEM AREAS; EVALUATION OF INITIAL EIGHTEEN MONTHS; WHERE DO WE GO FROM HERE?

A discussion of problem areas uncovered by the Council would fall into four main areas:

1. The problems of the hard-core unemployed and the under-privileged continue in the main to be treated with single one-shot remedies. Continuing efforts need to be made to link together a wide variety of programs to treat the illness instead of the symptoms. Persons in the above two categories need counseling and often health care, in addition to basic education, training, and placement. Many of these resources are now available but need to be brought together in a chain.

2. Minority group problems continue to be among the most distressing in and out of the labor force. Of particular concern is the general inability of minority group members to enter apprenticeships with labor unions; many find it difficult to find employment with contractors. The problems of women are equally distressing in the areas of equal wages, advancement, and opportunity to enter traditionally "male" occupations. This perhaps is as true among college educated women as it is among those with high school educations.

3. Older citizens continue to leave the labor force and to enter into an ambiguous existence which in some cases robs life of its meaningfulness. Older citizens need to be trained and brought into service occupations—where there is a great unmet need. Therefore, preretirement counseling centers have been suggested as one approach to dealing with this problem, perhaps utilizing the wide range of resources available in colleges and universities and coupling them with resources already available but unlinked.

4. Rural citizens, particularly youth, continue to have special prob-

lems in Iowa. The continuing decline in farm occupations means new opportunities will have to be made available to those in rural areas. An outreach system has been suggested to convey apprenticeship and training information to rural areas; in addition, vocational counseling needs to be strengthened. Area Vocational Schools will bring new training opportunities to rural youth, but the opportunities will be of no avail if information about them is not disseminated widely.

An evaluation of the work of the Council since its inception reveals strengths and weaknesses:

Coordination

As a system coordination has worked well but it will not become a smooth process until more is done at the federal level. "Creative federalism" will tend to help overcome weaknesses by eliminating certain bureaucratic procedures and by allowing states and regions to move forward toward meeting their own special and particular needs. Iowa is moving toward this approach but it will not be smooth until state reorganization is accomplished.

Liaison

The Council has achieved excellent results in this area by staying in close touch with Washington officials and with representatives at the regional level. The Council has been able to use a number of resources in this area which are unavailable to some other agencies—extensive travel, and perhaps closer relationships because of the quasi-federal nature of the Council. Continued contact with upper echelon Washington officials has given Iowa a distinct advantage in applying for federal funds in relation to other states.

Technical Assistance

The Council has been successful in this area with some limitations. One suggestion is that federal guidelines and regulations need to be made lucid and understandable enough that they can be comprehended at the local level. Even in local communities where guidelines are understood, confusion ensues anyway because guidelines are changed so often.

Information

This is a continuous function of the Council that has been successful to some extent but requires more work and constant attention. Newspaper coverage has been generally favorable but limited in scope. The Council's OJT project and work with minorities received excellent notice in the mass media, but a general and continuing understanding of the function and role of the Council has been lacking. More information needs to be made available to target group leaders—perhaps through newsletters and occasional intrastate regional meetings.

Special Projects

The Council has had a number of successful operations in this area, the most notable perhaps being the OJT projects. More creativity and innovation in state operations are needed. Better coordination perhaps will bring about imaginative special projects, and better information might lead to better coordination.

An overall evaluation of the Manpower Development Council raises some important questions:
1. Do we need a Manpower Development Council? The answer to this question seems to be "Yes." Even with efficient and productive state government organization, it will still be necessary to have both a coordinator and a planner.
2. Should all 50 states have Manpower Development Councils? The answer here seems to be "No." They are necessary as part of overall human resource development programs, but regional approaches would be more efficient than limited programs within each state.

Weaknesses which are the most readily apparent include the "weakest-link-in-the-chain" effect. It is difficult to move faster than other agencies. Salary restrictions and personnel "raiding" restrictions within state government retard maximum efforts. Observing political preserves when hiring personnel—a handicap in many states—is limiting.

Two liabilities can be seen—the short-term contract (18 months) and problems of having to deal with an agency with a "finite" life. The shortness of the contract makes good planning difficult. Other agencies are aware of the shortness of the life of the Council and do not react as effectively as they would, perhaps, to a permanent agency or to one with a life of three or more years.

Strengths of the Council include the establishment of the value of planning—coordinated and continuous planning, using all available data and resources.

The training of personnel in Iowa who have developed expertise in manpower areas is of great value. The staff has been aggressive and creative, yet has proved itself able to work with other agencies—some of them quite old-line organizations—and has brought together agencies which previously did not work together.

The Council has also provided the Governor with a "listening post" which better enables his staff to stay in touch with emerging patterns and programs in manpower and human resource development.

✹

The Concept and Problems
of Human Resources Development

✹

HAROLD L. SHEPPARD

THE NOTION OF HUMAN RESOURCES DEVELOPMENT IN OUR COUNTRY IS actually an old one; only the term is new.

At various times in our history, our country has expressed a concrete interest in education—education of a sort that is designed by intent to change individuals, primarily for some general or specific national purpose. The nineteenth century beginnings of the public school system in America, the earlier Northwest Ordinance setting aside a given ratio of tracts for schools, the Morrill Act creating our great system of land-grant colleges during the last century, the G.I. bills starting at the end of World War II, and the National Defense Education Act in the late 1950's are evidence of the importance we have attached to the development of human resources. We have been practicing human resources development for generations, without necessarily knowing the name of the game we give it today.

The recent emergence of a national, conscious interest in what

HAROLD L. SHEPPARD is a social scientist at the W. E. Upjohn Institute for Employment Research, Washington, D.C.

we now call the development of human resources does have something special about it. In the first place, thanks to the important analyses of such men as Theodore Schultz, starting from his days in Iowa, we have come to appreciate that our economic growth is not some simple product of investments in capital goods alone—that indeed our economic growth has become more and more attributable to investments in what we now call human capital. Now that we recognize and appreciate this fact, we have moved to a more conscious, deliberate attempt to formulate policies and to design programs to direct and enlarge investments in human beings, as one of the major means of assuring economic growth. As one writer has put it:

> The economy's output may be raised not only by increasing the supply of inputs . . . or by technological change . . . but also by numerous kinds of alterations in the *qualities* of the inputs of a sort which typically escape the scrutiny of the economic theorist. It is apparent that economic development is associated with important qualitative changes in the human agent as a factor of production. These improvements take such forms as changes in knowledge, technical skills, organizational and managerial abilities, levels of economic aspiration, responsiveness to economic incentives, and capacity to undertake and adapt to innovation. The nature of the mechanisms by which these alterations take place is as yet only very imperfectly understood.[1]

We do not yet know or understand perfectly how such improvements take place or how they can be consciously brought about, but it is here that sociologists and psychologists have a contribution to make if they were to take on some responsibility to do so.

Our concern with the development of human resources, however, cannot be said to be exclusively a result of new discoveries in academic knowledge and research, important as those discoveries may be. A second and perhaps more important reason for this concern is related to some very practical experiences our country has had in attempting to implement and administer the new programs starting with the administration of John F. Kennedy and continuing with that of Lyndon B. Johnson. While many economists were arguing either for or against the doctrine that our recent high unemployment rates were due to a deficiency in aggregate demand, and for or against the other doctrine that the high rates were due to structural problems, Congress went ahead in its

[1] Nathan Rosenberg, "Neglected Dimensions in the Analysis of Economic Change," in *Explorations in Social Change*, edited by George K. Zollschax and Walter Hirsch (New York: Houghton Mifflin Co., 1964), pp. 652–53.

pragmatic fashion and pushed legislation based on *both* doctrines. The tax credit for capital investment and the substantial reduction in the income tax were major efforts to increase the aggregate demand for goods and thus for labor. But in addition to such acts, Congress proceeded to pass a large number of bills designed to attack the so-called structural obstacles to full employment. These bills included the Area Redevelopment Act (suceeded by the Public Works and Economic Development Act of 1965); the Manpower Development and Training Act of 1962; the Vocational Education Act of 1963; the Appalachian Regional Development Act of 1965; and the Economic Opportunity Act of 1964, the "war against poverty," to name the major programs. We should also add the equal employment opportunities provisions of the 1964 Civil Rights Act.

All of these pieces of legislation were based on the conviction that it is not enough to raise the general, national level of purchasing power in order to cut rates of unemployment. The general demand of private industry and employers for labor cannot be completely satisfied if we have thousands of job-seekers who simply are not qualified to meet the skill requirements of the jobs being opened up as a result of increases in the demand for more employees. This demand cannot be met if thousands of men and women do not live where the demand exists. Young high school graduates and high school dropouts are not going to be hired, at least not for long, if their work habits and attitudes are not congruent with the demands of the modern workplace. And thousands of American citizens cannot find jobs if some employers entertain irrelevant prejudices against them because of skin color, national origin, or religion.

The lack of adequate skills and work attitudes, living in the wrong place, and prejudice—to name a few noneconomic variables— can exert a pressure on rates of employment, even in the midst of a general demand for more labor in our factories and offices.

Now that we have this vast array of legislative weapons to facilitate economic growth and to reduce unemployment, now that thousands of dedicated administrators are trying to implement the new programs, we face a new level of challenges that bring us face to face with the unsolved problems of our society and economy. The fiscal and monetary policies of the early 1960's were necessary, and so were such programs as MDTA. They still are necessary, but are they sufficient to reach the objectives of full economic and social growth?

The area redevelopment programs were designed in large part to provide rather liberal, long-term, low-interest loans to private industry in those parts of the country with chronic and substantial unemployment or underemployment (as measured by low incomes). But in administering such worthy programs, many of us discovered that if the businessmen and other community leaders no longer had any entrepreneurial orientation in their personal and social outlook, all the "easy money" in the world could not produce applications for loans to finance expansions or new industries.

If the local community (or even the local area made up of a few counties) was so afflicted by lack of purpose and unity in their everyday community and governmental activities, the necessary organizational arrangements as a prerequisite for a loan would be missing. This is true of any regional development approach that attempts a multicounty or interstate scheme.

In many depressed areas the work force has either been depleted of its skilled manpower through outmigration to other areas of economic opportunity or is no longer capable of or interested in supporting an adequate vocational education system because of its weak tax base and because of a spirit of demoralization and resignation. Large parts of the Appalachian region fit this picture, and if the benefits of a vast highway system now being programmed for that region are to be witnessed in our lifetime, the development of the human resources in Appalachia warrants equally urgent attention.

Inadequate managerial and entrepreneurial talent, lack of community organization for purposes of economic growth, and deficiencies in the school system are examples of what is included in the list of sufficient conditions for the restoration of large parts of those populations located in various areas of our nation. But the concept of depressed areas can be applied to more than the agricultural Deep South, the Upper Peninsula of Michigan, or Appalachia. Until recently many program policies have been governed not by reality but by the statistical average approach to large urban metropolitan areas. When the Department of Labor used the term "Detroit" or "Los Angeles," for example, these words referred to statistical artifacts, to the total standard metropolitan area covering two or more counties, possibly with hundreds of square miles. For such areas, the average unemployment rate could be so low or the average family income figure could be so high as to convey the impression that in every *part* of a given area these figures were virtually identical.

The statistical average approach to a megalopolis can fool us into believing that Los Angeles (and I use that name only as an illustration of my principle) has a very low rate of unemployment and a high family income and that, therefore, things are humming beautifully.

The Watts uprisings One and Two showed the fallacy of the unqualified usefulness of the homogeneous labor market area concept. More recent outbreaks have only confirmed the fallacy. For years we have been complacently diagnosing and prescribing on the basis of a statistical thermometer that registered the net *sum* of the pluses and minuses of our social body, which blinded us to the existence and location of the minuses, the fevers in a part of that body.

Depressed areas can and do exist in our urban centers, and they can be eradicated only partly through urban renewal as we now use that term. *Human* renewal must become the object of our imagination, our brains, our money, and our organizational talents.

The Moynihan Report was one honest, candid effort to point out the need for the redevelopment of the human resources in one part of our American society—namely, a significant minority, and only a minority, of Negro urban Americans. Moynihan advocated a program to *supplement*—not to replace—the Civil Rights Acts, the Manpower Development and Training Act, and the Economic Opportunity Act.

We know enough in the social sciences to conclude that economic development requires, among other things, a strong psychological bent toward achievement and persistence toward success among an active entrepreneurial class—even in noncapitalistic societies. It is also true that occupational and social mobility among the rest of a population structure is partly dependent upon the same socio-psychological factors. Workers in the lower social strata exhibiting these characteristics typically seek out and take advantage of those opportunities that lead to or constitute upward economic and social mobility.

One important point in the Moynihan Report is that achievement motivation is strongest among the sons in low-income families which have *both* a father and a mother present—whether they be Negroes in urban ghettos or whites in West Virginia and Kentucky.

If we are really serious about a comprehensive program of human resource development, we cannot continue to run away from those aspects of our problems which relate to the socio-psychological dimension. The emphasis on this dimension is not a substitute for all the more easily accepted programs having to do with vocational training and retraining, regional economic development, and our fiscal and monetary policies. The emphasis is on one more

additional set of factors that must be coped with in order to raise
the probability of success of those programs and policies.

Regardless of what we might think of the success so far of
Operation Head Start in the war against poverty program, we
should nevertheless view its intellectual justification in these very
terms—as an effort to "intervene" as early as possible in the emo-
tional and cognitive experiences of persons now living in poverty
so that they might be able to participate effectively in the structure
of opportunities presumably created through our educational, economic, and governmental processes. Of course it should also be
obvious that the entire educational system needs to be adapted and
changed to cope with the products of successful Head Start projects.

Since the Moynihan Report, a much more ambitious study has
been completed, dealing with the issue of equal educational opportunities, sponsored by the U.S. Office of Education, and directed by
James Coleman of Johns Hopkins University. When this report
has been adequately digested and translated from its highly technical language and sophisticated statistical analyses, it will probably
cause just as much of a stir as the Moynihan Report.

There are some findings in the Coleman Report that may not
be surprising to the general public or to most educational authorities, such as (1) "minority children have a serious educational deficiency at the start of school; and (2) they have an even more serious
deficiency at the end of school, which is obviously in part a result
of school."[2]

But what may be surprising, and perhaps even disturbing, are
the following points:

> First, within each racial group, the strong relation of family economic
> and educational background to achievement does not diminish over
> the period of school, and may even increase over the elementary years.
> Second, most of the variation in student achievement lies within the
> same school, very little of it is between schools. The implication of
> these last two results is clear: family background differences account
> for much more variation in achievement than do school differences.
>
> Even the school-to-school variation in achievement, though rela-
> tively small, is itself almost wholly due to the *social* environment pro-
> vided by the school: the educational backgrounds and aspirations of
> other students in the school, and the educational backgrounds and at-
> tainments of the teachers in the school. *Per pupil expenditure, books
> in the library, and a host of other facilities and curricular measures*

[2] James S. Coleman, "Equal Schools or Equal Students?" *The Public Interest,* Summer, 1966, pp. 72–73. Subsequent quotations are from this article.

show virtually no relation to achievement if the "social" environment of the school—the educational backgrounds of other students and teachers—is held constant.

Altogether, the sources of inequality of educational opportunity appear to lie first in the home itself and the cultural influences immediately surrounding the home; then they lie in the schools' ineffectiveness to free achievement from the impact of the home, and in the schools' cultural homogeneity which perpetuates the social influences of the home and its environs.

Pointing more explicitly to the role of socio-psychological factors, Coleman writes:

One final result of the survey gives an indication of still another—and perhaps the most important—element necessary for equality of educational opportunity for Negroes. One attitude of students was measured at grades 9 and 12—an attitude which indicated the degree to which the student felt in control of his own fate. . . . Negroes much less often than whites had such a sense of control of their fate—a difference which corresponds directly to reality, and which corresponds even more markedly to the Negro's historical position in American society. However, despite the very large achievement differences between whites and Negroes at the 9th and 12th grades, those Negroes who gave responses indicating a sense of control of their own fate achieved higher on the tests than those whites who gave the opposite responses. This attitude was more highly related to achievement than any other factor in the student's background or school.

This result suggests that internal changes in the Negro, changes in his conception of himself in relation to his environment, may have more effect on Negro achievement than any other single factor. The determination to overcome relevant obstacles, and the belief that he will overcome them . . . may be the most crucial elements in achieving equality of opportunity—not because of changes they will create in the white community, but principally because of the changes they create in the Negro himself.

These considerations are not of strictly academic research interest. Coleman is saying that the crucial criterion is not merely how equal are the number of books in school buildings and the age of the buildings, "not on what resources go into education, but on what product comes out," what the results are in verbal and mathematical achievements, for example, that a young person has when he or she enters into competition in the labor market. And the monumental study he directed for the Office of Education (entitled "Equality of Educational Opportunity") indicates that family influences and self-conception explain much more of the variations in these achievements than any other set of factors.

The challenge in the years to come will be not primarily to conduct more and more research but rather to seek those techniques, those methods and new programs that can be used to improve such things as family structure and human motivation and self-conceptions. Economists such as Adam Smith, John Stuart Mill, and Theodore Schultz have tried to tell us that economics must include the variable of human capital, and this applies to the analysis not only of underdeveloped countries but to the developed ones as well. Economic phenomena cannot be adequately comprehended through the use of economic variables alone; *non*-economic variables are also involved, which was the lesson of Max Weber.

Now the challenge is to develop those techniques, those "intervention strategies," that will strengthen our ability to change those noneconomic factors that stand in the way of a fruitful development of our human resources.

✳

The Economist and Human Resource Development

✳

J. EARL WILLIAMS

THEODORE SCHULTZ PIONEERED WHEN, IN HIS PRESIDENTIAL ADDRESS TO the American Economics Association in 1960, he said:

> The failure to treat human resources explicitly as a form of capi-
> tal, as a produced means of production, as the product of investment,
> has fostered the retention of the classical notion of labor as a capacity
> to do manual work requiring little knowledge and skill, a capacity
> with which, according to this notion, laborers are endowed about
> equally. This notion of labor was wrong in the classical period and it
> is patently wrong now.[1]

Harbison and Myers, in their book *Education, Manpower, and
Economic Growth,*[2] go beyond this beginning by noting and agree-
ing with the interdisciplinary contributions of those traditionally
known as the "educationists" as well as relating human resource

---

J. EARL WILLIAMS is Professor of Economics and Director of the Human
Resources Institute, University of Houston, Houston, Tex.

[1] Theodore W. Schultz, "Investment in Human Capital," *The American
Economic Review*, Vol. 51, No. 1, p. 3, Mar. 1961.

[2] Frederick Harbison and Charles A. Myers, *Education, Manpower, and
Economic Growth: Strategies of Human Resource Development*, New York: Mc-
Graw-Hill, 1964.

development to economic development. It is often the "education-ist" who has argued that human resources determine the subsequent nature and behavior of society. Further, from an economic stand-point we must have human resource development to provide the knowledge, skills, and incentive for a productive economy. In the final analysis, it takes human beings to mobilize capital, exploit re-sources, and create markets. It is merely a truism to say that a na-tion is underdeveloped because her people are underdeveloped and that ultimately the wealth of a nation stems from the power to de-velop and utilize the capacities of the people. Consequently many economists recognize that human resource development is a pre-requisite to economic growth with a monumental though perhaps immeasurable return.

Unfortunately, most economists do not concern themselves nearly so much with the human factors of production but are pri-marily concerned with academic debating (confined almost solely to each other) that the human problem is one of ineffective demand or structural unemployment. At least this recognizes the problem which is far better than those who wave their wands of abstraction in dramatic insistence that any investment by government must re-sult in some vaguely defined economic return. Rather than deal in such broad generalities, it would be far better to deal with specific investments. When these specifics are discussed, it is far easier to see that, costly though some of the injections may be, the return is in the form of eliminating a human resource from the government welfare rolls and adding him to the tax-paying rolls. A few ex-amples should suffice:

1. The Department of Labor recently announced that the average trainee in an OJT program recovered the cost of his training with his new or additional taxes within a period of two years.
2. A program designed to make it possible for a newly trained worker to move to where the job is located may appear to be costly, but it may be the only way to start this resource on the road to tax-paying citizenship.
3. It is necessary to look at the socio-psychological dimension. The more hard-core the problem, the more the dimensions must be considered and the more expensive the cure will be. It is be-coming increasingly necessary in these cases to develop a team composed of counselors, social workers, teachers, and recruiters. Some authorities feel that this team must discover all of the cul-tural gaps and problems of each individual trainee and build into his training environment the missing links which are needed for training and employment of a human resource in modern society. This would of course result in a high per capita cost.

but when you look at the alternative of generations of the same families on welfare, the cost is small indeed.

4. The special emphasis given to the problem of human resource development of the Negro population is evidence that structural unemployment problems still exist and is a stark reminder that the failure to properly develop and utilize these resources is a real cost to society. In those cases where prejudice relegates the Negro to work only at certain jobs and at certain rates of pay, an added real cost is that it condemns white people to work in less efficient firms, businessmen to sell to poorer customers, and communities to skimp on essential public services because they cannot afford any better.

The technological revolution is adding a second structural factor to the problem of Negro unemployment in the form of higher educational requirements. This mitigates against equal employment opportunities in that the educational level of the Negro is less than that for whites, particularly in the South. Consequently, while the unemployment level for whites has been decreasing in recent months, it has been increasing for Negroes to the extent that Negro unemployment is now two and a half times the rate for whites. This kind of situation emphasizes the importance of a sense of control of their own fate. Work force participation rates are evidence that the male Negro often finds himself so devoid of any feeling of control of his fate that he gives up entirely. For example, despite the fact that the working age population of male Negroes in the South increased during the 1950's, their participation rate declined by more than 10 percent. This is not explained by increased participation in education. That the educational handicap is related to this is revealed by the fact that labor force participation of white females in the South in the 1950's increased by more than 22 percent. The existence of this problem on a national scale is indicated in a special Department of Labor survey made in slums of major cities in March, 1966, which discovered 150,000 Negro males in the age group 25–64 who had lost hope and were no longer looking for jobs. There is little doubt that the full development and utilization of Negro human resources is an economic problem of major proportions which must be solved if the economy is to realize its growth potential.

It is long past time for economists to realize that expenditures can be and are made by the government for purposes other than a balanced economy per se and that an economy is imbalanced because its human resources are imbalanced. They have not been properly developed, or fully utilized, or fully compensated, or adequately trained.

The teacher then should be concerned with each of the individual pieces which go to make up the whole, no matter how small. He should be concerned that, even in this day of greater enlightenment regarding human resources, more money is spent to solve the problems of migrant birds than those of migrant farmers. A careful analysis of human resource problems is thus a requisite for an intelligent evaluation of governmental expenditures.

Finally, there is a need for a broader role in human resource development by the universities. This approach must be interdisciplinary. This may be one reason for the fear some economists have of becoming involved with human resource problems. They soon discover that sociologists, psychologists, educationists, social work academicians, political scientists, and many others have roles to play.

The university can perform a valuable service by giving technical aid to groups concerned with human resource problems. This may be in the form of program information and development, assistance in operation, or evaluation. Further, human resource programs have developed so quickly that most of those filling positions do not have the broad interdisciplinary background required. Consequently, training and orientation programs should be developed by the university. This same logic applies to the graduate of the university who has a whole range of new job possibilities in the human resource field and who would be far better prepared if he had a basic background in human resources. Finally, more policy-oriented research is needed. Since the economist generally claims that one of his major roles is to influence policy related to the economic system, this is another way of saying he should try to influence policies concerned with the economic welfare of the nation.

Thus the economist can make a real contribution to human resource development by becoming a part of a university-wide interdisciplinary approach to the problems. Throughout his teaching and university services, there should be the basic realization that there is, or should be, an interconnection of anything as small as a single OJT program, established to solve a human resource problem going through the fiscal pipelines as an identifiable expenditure, and a balanced economy. Greater satisfaction should be derived too from the fact that this concern with a better development and allocation of human resources reduces the likelihood of another serious imbalance. By translating this concern into action, we will have taken an interdisciplinary approach to the solution of a major economic problem.

✻

Social Justice Aspects
of Human Resources Development

✻

AUSTIN E. MILLER, S.J.

HUMAN RENEWAL MUST BECOME THE OBJECT OF OUR IMAGINATION, our brain, our money, and our organizational genius. This development and treatment by the economist, the sociologist, the educator, and the psychologist in the United States is both new and old. The enduring pursuits of freedom and education and the persistent drive for justice have ever marked our country.

So it is not altogether new that we are interested in human resources. Throughout the history of our country, however, we seem to have emphasized the development of the physical resources, the purely economic resources. We did not have in mind ultimately that through the development of these economic resources we would thereby be benefiting human beings. This idealism may have been lacking because there has not been sufficient emphasis on the non-physical features. Internal improvements, a big political issue of the mid-nineteenth century was development not so much of men but of physical resources. To bridge the East with the West by

REV. AUSTIN E. MILLER, S.J., is Chairman of the Social Order Conference, Creighton University, Omaha, Neb., and Chairman of the Great Plains States Regional Manpower Advisory Committee.

canals, roads, rivers, harbors—even to settle this West here in Iowa, breadbasket of the nation perhaps—the emphasis of primary importance has been on the development of the land, the farm. the mines, and the forests.

We could be prouder of this development if the theme running throughout had been in the area of developing human resources as well. Fortunately the more recent manpower program that we are tackling has a sort of a national consensus. This emphasis on the development of human resources is now popular, it is patriotic. it is the thing to do, it is good Americanism. It is religious—Jew. Gentile, Christian, or non-Christian swept along in it—because it includes the principal tenets of the world's religions. It is wise, it is common sensical. Everybody now sees that the pragmatic aspect of it really fits in with our common-sense attitude that we should be interested in human resources. It is democratic, crossing lines of class, race, and creed. It is more direct, more affirmative, more positive, more constructive. There is an honesty with which we approach it. It is not extracurricular, not just a by-product of other disciplines, not just an afterthought. This is our real earnest position. Members of the Manpower Development Training Advisory Committee throughout the nation are trying to discern the needs of the underemployed and the unemployed, the dropout, the minority group, the poverty-stricken, and thus adapt the organization and structure thereto. It is a person-to-person treatment, it is client-oriented.

Now it is necessary to implement the human resource programs that we have spent a decade or two discussing, evolving, developing, probing, and testing. We have had a great deal of legislation—ARA, MDTA, EOA, and the rest of them—and we may have more, but hopefully the proliferation has ceased and some coordination may emerge.

A very important aspect of human resources development—the propulsion energy in the program—is social justice. This obligationism, social justice, is the virtue which inclines each of us to contribute to the common good. It is outgoing, it is that which makes one think of others. It arises from our very makeup and our very being. It is always urging its expression to go out and seek to help the group of which we are a part, to better someone, to better another group. All parts must be harmonized within a group, and these parts—whether they be servants or master, citizens or leaders. followers or those who blaze the trail—all have this particular virtue or this particular obligation to seek a common good, the public welfare. Hence there are 170 million people beginning to be worried about 20 million of another color of skin. Hence there are educators who are not just academic bureaucrats but are interested in relating their findings, their research, their thought processes and expression thereof (by papers, seminars, study clubs, and discussions) to everyday life so as to help man become a better and more successful part of society.

Social justice is the key to coordinating, directing, inspiring the whole gamut of human resource development. Legislatures practice it both in the halls of Congress and in the state legislatures. When they pass laws, when the administrative branch executes law, when the judicial branch reviews and adjudicates matters of law, they are all practicing social justice insofar as they are contributing to the common good.

Each of us has the power, the obligation to contribute to the common good. Economists and labor consultants, sociologists and educators, as well as psychologists contribute their particular observations and findings concerning the natural sciences in the development of human resources; but it will bog down if it is prompted by selfish interest. Today we have a situation, a condition, a way of life that is outgoing-minded, that is social justice-minded. Human society is so integrated that we cannot help feeling motivated toward this drive that has positivism. Fortunately it is also constructive, not destructive. We are not intending to do away with benefits received from a former heritage of economists and sociologists. We are not trying to scrap the whole economic system of social order. We are trying to put a little warmth of human kindness with cold scientific organizational and structural changes, good legislation, good persuasion, personal participation, and group action.

CHAPTER 4

✸

Human Resources Development as a Learning Process

✸

KENNETH E. BOULDING

THE GENERAL PROBLEM OF DEVELOPMENT IN SOCIETY CANNOT BE CON-sidered except as development in all its forms—political, cultural, artistic, and moral as well as economic. The development of society is essentially a continuation of the evolutionary process that began with the first big bang of creation or whatever it was that started developing the elements, then went on to life, on to man, and then on to society. I regard biological and social evolution as essentially a single process, though social evolution is more complicated simply because of the complexity of man himself. All development and evolution involve the learning process because the only thing that can evolve is knowledge or information, in the sense of the improbability of structures. I think of knowledge as the capital stock of information and information as an improbable arrangement of something. You and I are among the more improbable things in the universe; the more we know the less probable we get.

KENNETH E. BOULDING is Professor of Economics at the University of Michigan, Ann Arbor, Mich., and President-elect of the American Economics Association.

Matter in the form of the chemical elements did not seem to evolve much after the first twenty minutes of the universe until man got into the game and started making new elements. Apart from nuclear transformations matter is conserved and so is energy, and even including nuclear transformations matter and energy taken together are conserved. Obviously, therefore, neither matter nor energy can evolve. Energy is not even conserved in the sense that the deplorable second law of thermodynamics, which nobody seems to have been able to repeal, states—that energy gets less and less available. Thus, if we are going to have evolution the only thing that can evolve is complexity of structure, which is almost the same thing as knowledge. In this sense, helium "knows more" than hydrogen, and all the other steps follow from this.

Looking at society from this evolutionary point of view we can see human learning as an evolutionary process. It is a process essentially of mutation and selection. Mutation creates new images through the imagination, and the critical faculties, including the senses, select those which are most valuable. Before the advent of the human nervous system, mutation, as far as we know, was random. Since the development of the human nervous system, evolution has been going on inside the human head probably faster than outside it, and soon the evolution inside the head begins to affect the world outside it.

The advent of man therefore signaled an acceleration in the evolutionary process in this part of the universe. This has not been the only acceleration; as we look at the history of evolution it seems clear it goes into higher gear every so often and the intervals between these gear changes become fewer. This may, of course, be an illusion because of something that is happening to the nature of time, but that is speculative.

Economic development is also a mutation-selection process. Commodities are species, just like animals. They are indeed animals which have a genetic apparatus consisting of human society. The automobile is obviously a large four-wheeled bug with a detachable brain that entered the ecological system about sixty years ago. It has displaced the horse, and if we are not careful it may displace people. The main biological difference between an automobile and a horse is that the genetics of an automobile are more complicated. Despite appearances to the contrary, Ford's Mustang is not produced by sexual union between a Thunderbird and a Plymouth, but it is produced in a womb, that is, a factory, and it is conceived in the mind of an engineer. Commodities are born through production, they die in consumption, and they form a population. They form an ecological system along with all other species. Like biological species they can be eliminated in competition for food, in this case the money of the consumer, and they then become extinct like the bustle.

Economic development, then, is not just having an excess of production over consumption, and it is certainly not piling up agricultural surpluses. It involves a mutation of commodities into more and more complex forms, that is, into objects which have more knowledge embodied in them. Thus, the microphone, for instance, is an extremely improbable arrangement of matter, much less probable than the speaking trumpet which might have been used a hundred years ago. It is here because of mutations and selections which went on in the human mind. All capital, indeed, is frozen knowledge, that is, human knowledge imposed on a material world.

Knowledge in the mind is not only prior to capital, that is, knowledge in matter, but it is very much superior to it. We can see this very clearly if we look at the development of Japan in the last twenty years by contrast with the development of Indonesia. In Japan the material capital was largely destroyed in 1945; nevertheless it took only a few years to get all the material capital back, even in improved form, because the human capital (that is, the image in the mind which created it) was still there. In fact, the human capital of Japan was probably improved by defeat. It seems to be a fundamental principle of development that nothing fails like success, because the more successful you are the less you learn from it. In the case of Japan, the military defeat acted as a kind of shock treatment, curing its political mental ill health, and as a result it has made a world's record for economic development in the last twenty years, growing at the rate of about 8 percent per annum per capita. This fantastic record is almost wholly the result of the extraordinary capacity of the Japanese for learning. They seem to have very few psychological obstacles to learning of the kind that bedevil us. There seems to be something in our culture that holds us back. Our rate of development has averaged not more than 3 percent, and in recent years, in some areas of the economy, we even seem to have some technological decline, as anyone who has ridden on a railroad lately or even mailed a letter can testify. It looks almost as if in some fields our rate of forgetting has exceeded our rate of learning.

Some interesting conclusions can be drawn from this view of development as learning and of learning as a mutation-selection process. Thus, there are some things which have a survival value in the long run which do not have survival value in the short run. Economists are familiar with this interesting problem under the heading of the infant industry argument. Biologists are familiar with the same problem in what might be called the Sewell Wright principle of the optimum degree of cellulation. If too many species are in contact and if competition is too intense, this will slow down the rate of evolution, because all mutations will be adverse. There is a strong probability anyway that most mutations will be adverse, because obviously if you are where you are you must have gotten there because you survived. "You must be all right, Jack, and anywhere you go from where you are is bad." This is biological conservatism, or what might be called the republican view of evolution, that all mutations are for the worse. The trouble is that probably 99.4 percent of mutations *are* for the worse. Only a small fraction of mutations are for the better, and in a way the more the system has survived the less likely is it to suffer change. One of the problems we face in economic development is the appalling stability of low-level societies, like the Indian village, which has an astonishingly stable equilibrium. Outside agencies try to disturb it, but when they go away it all goes back the way it was before.

The moral of all this is that in any kind of social development process it is human knowledge that is predominant, simply for the reason that human beings are brighter than other animals, and even the brightest commodities that they produce are dumb. If you leave an automobile to itself it will run off the road. Even the brightest computers probably do not reach the native intelligence of the one-year-old human. It is the human organism, therefore—this very peculiar nonlinear computer produced by largely unskilled labor—which is the real clue to social evolution.

One of the most astonishing facts about the growth of human knowledge is that all human knowledge is lost every generation and has to be transmitted to a new set of minds. It sounds rather shocking to say this so bluntly, but the only place that human knowledge exists is in human heads. There is no knowledge in a library. If all the humans died off, the library could not do a thing. The books would just sit there and rot. There is a curious illusion among scientists that knowledge exists in the bindings of scientific periodicals, but this is not true. If it does not exist in the mind it exists nowhere, and the rate of consumption of knowledge is appalling because of the short length of human life. This is perhaps why the great acceleration in the rate of social evolution took place with the development of agriculture. Agriculture is the key to all subsequent development, because it probably increased the span of human life by five to ten years, as we moved from the paleolithic to the neolithic. This, of course, is speculation, as records do not exist. It is hard to believe, however, that improved food supplies and greater security, stable settlements and moderately comfortable houses did not increase the expectation of life by at least five to ten years. This would be enough to set off an irreversible process of the accumulation of knowledge, because now the human race could learn more in every generation than it lost by death.

Thus the key to all accelerations in the rate of social evolution is to be found in new methods of transmitting knowledge between generations. In traditional society the main transmission belt is the family, especially the grandmother. One of the problems of economic development is that this transmission belt has to be broken and new methods of transmission through the school, the library, the mass media, and so on have to be introduced. It is not surprising that this introduces certain traumatic experiences in the early stages of development. You have to teach people that what they learned at their mother's knee is largely nonsense. It is not surprising that economic development is tough and that economists who go around giving good advice about it are not always delighted by the reception they get.

Another interesting proposition that is derived from the evolutionary point of view is in regard to the probability of the stationary state. The interesting thing about the stationary state is that it is always on the way and never comes. This has been happening now for four billion years, and we can justifiably get a little tired waiting for it. Any given method of transmitting knowledge would eventually produce a stationary state, simply because the greater the stock of knowledge, the greater its consumption in every generation by loss through death. The larger the body of knowledge, therefore, the larger the proportion of resources that have to be put into the knowledge industry just to maintain it; and the stationary state arrives at the point where the maintenance of existing knowledge takes all the available resources of the society.

There have been many societies which have exhibited something which looks like a temporary stationary state. China may have been an example for a considerable period, and certainly many of the so-called primitive societies have looked like this. Primitive societies, of course, are never as primitive as they look at first sight. They frequently have a very large stock of rather useless knowledge, and they do not develop because they have to put an enormous amount into reproducing useless or even pernicious magical knowledge. We put a lot into this sort of thing also, but we seem to have something to spare. Even though the increase in the stock of knowledge enables us to produce it faster, there may be some sort of diminishing returns here. Hence the rising rate of consumption of knowledge eventually overtakes the falling rate of production of knowledge, and we have a stationary state in which production equals the consumption and there cannot be any increase. Everything then goes into education, nothing into research and development.

According to one estimate, the knowledge industry in this country absorbs now about 30 percent of the gross national product. The rate of increase of knowledge is still so great that it certainly doubles every generation and in some fields seems to double about every fifteen years. If there were no further improvements in the methods of transmitting or creating knowledge, the business of simply replacing existing knowledge every generation could grow until perhaps by the middle of the next century it would absorb the whole knowledge industry and the increase of knowledge would grind to a halt. We would have enormous universities devoted wholly to preserving what we already know. Research would disappear because there would be nobody to do it. We would all be teaching like mad just to transmit this enormous body of knowledge into the next generation, unless, of course, we have another mutation in the teaching process.

Nonetheless, this seems to be what has always happened to the evolutionary process, and this is the only reason that the universe has not come to a stationary state long ago. One would think offhand that it has had plenty of time, some six or ten billion years. If the stationary state has not been reached, it is because of these mutations in the methods of transmitting and acquiring knowledge. Sex, incidentally, was an early one of these mutations, which might now almost be disappearing with the development of self-conscious genetics. We may be on the threshold of great changes in the teaching process at the moment, involving teaching machines, learning drugs, or even perhaps a surgical operation for the differential calculus. If this happens the stationary state is postponed still further.

One of the depressing things about economic development is the scarcity of it, in spite of the fact that we seem to put considerable resources into it. It is very disheartening to go back to Adam Smith on this subject, but we do not seem to have improved on it very much in almost 200 years. Just by way of illustration, therefore, I am applying the evolutionary approach to two problems in economic development which have produced a large number of

Ph.D. theses but up to now very little enlightenment. The first is the question of whether we ought to have balanced growth or unbalanced growth. The evolutionary approach suggests that there are some activities in which knowledge has a kind of multiplier, and it is these activities we want to stress. We clearly do not want to increase knowledge equally in all parts of society and in all industries. In the early stages of development it is clear that there are very large payoffs to the increase of knowledge in agriculture. These payoffs are to the society at large rather than to agriculture itself, because the increase of knowledge in agriculture tends to make agriculture unprofitable and chases people out of it.

We have now reached the point where agriculture is only 5 percent of the gross national product. It may be, therefore, that research and development in agriculture are not very important any more, simply because they cannot release much in the way of resources to go into other things. It is now these other things which have the larger potential for multiplying knowledge. One of the interesting things about development is that those industries which are successful technologically will often tend to decline and the industries which are technologically stagnant, like haircutting and education, grow and grow. We may get to the point, therefore, where the technologically progressive industries are all very small and the stagnant ones are enormous. This is presumably when the process comes to an end.

We may be at a point where we need radical readjustments in the distribution of intellectual resources in this country, and the misallocation of these resources is becoming a serious problem. There is, therefore, a certain validity in the unbalanced growth thesis in the sense that as anything grows, its structure (that is, the proportions of its parts) has to change. We can never preserve the structure of a thing that is growing and we always have to be on the lookout for what structural changes are necessary. On the other hand, it is also true that there are certain syndromes of growth. Certain industries, for instance, tend to grow together, and if we neglect any particular element in such a syndrome this will affect adversely the growth of the whole. In other words we have to maintain a certain balance among the imbalances.

The second problem of economic development might be called the "Prebisch problem," after its most distinguished exponent. This is the argument that the poor countries, especially the Latin-American ones, are in sad shape because they produce primary products, and in the course of development the terms of trade turn against them. They have a parity problem, just like agriculture.

The argument is certainly not absurd. On the other hand, when one asks what can be done about it, apart from wringing hands and bemoaning and arguing with Dr. Tinbergen that the rich countries must simply make large grants to the poor ones, we do not seem to get very far.

What we must do here is to look at the dynamics of knowledge and ask the question, "Can a poor country that wants to get rich quick pick a winner in technological development and specialize in that?" This is, of course, hard to do, and I have come to the depressing conclusion that the only really good recipe for getting rich quick is to be lucky. This is an unfriendly and unpleasant thing to say to people because we have always believed that the way to get rich is to be virtuous. No matter how virtuous you are, however, if you back the wrong horse in your specializations you won't get rich. Many of the poor countries have been in this unfortunate position and only a few of them have really picked the winners.

Obviously if your terms of trade are bad you should not be producing what you are producing. The answer to bad terms of trade is to get out of your present occupation and produce something else. On the other hand, how do we know that what we are going to get into is going to be all right? The answer is, we do not. In the development of Japan, for instance, the terms of trade were quite important in the 1880's and 1890's, mainly because of an unexpected piece of luck. Japan was specializing in silk and the European silk industry was severely affected by disease, hence the Japanese had extraordinarily good terms of trade in silk for a whole generation. Though this was not a crucial factor in their development, it certainly helped. A similar example is Malaya, which has surprised everybody in the last twenty years. Twenty years ago Malaya looked like a hopeless case, but it has forged ahead whereas Indonesia has been going backwards, Burma has retreated into traditionalism, and Ceylon has torn itself apart with racial conflict. Part of the reason for this was that the Malayans were simply lucky. I am not sure how self-conscious they were about it, because they were producing rubber which everybody thought was going to be a drug on the market, especially with the development of synthetics. Actually they made a bet, as it were, that technologically biology was going to beat chemistry, and they turned out to be right. The decline in costs of natural rubber due to a rapidly advancing technology has more than outweighed the worsening of terms of trade. Even though they did not have very good terms of trade in the old sense, they were able to beat this through technological development. It does not really matter what your terms of trade are as long as you can reduce your costs fast enough. Whether the Malayans will be able to get away with this in the next twenty years is, of course, another matter.

These cases illustrate why the problems of economic development are so difficult, much more difficult, in fact, than most economists are willing to admit. The difficulties arise because all development involves decision-making under uncertainty, and indeed under very large uncertainty. If you have to make a decision under uncertainty, it is easy to make the wrong one. There is no rule which tells you how to make the right decision, even if you play the minimax and be very conservative. You may still make the wrong decision, and for the purpose of development a dangerous and unwise right decision may be the only thing which can really get a society off its launching pad, and the decent, conservative wrong decision may be disastrous. In development the minimax is not good enough. One may have to play the "maximax" and take decisions that will only pay off if you are lucky; that is, you have to be a plunger.

The development of the United States and the West has in some measure been due to a succession of lucky accidents. Perhaps we always did the right things and sometimes for the wrong reasons. We were lucky and so we got rich. There are many decisions that might have gone the other way and would have been disastrous. When one looks at history in these terms one gets an uneasy feeling about how long luck can continue.

Even if virtue cannot guarantee development, one has more confidence in the proposition that certain kinds of vice can prevent it. There are many countries (for instance Argentina) which have stopped an active developmental process because of foolish governmental policies, and it is certainly not inconceivable that we might do the same thing in this country.

[EDITORS' NOTE: In answer to a question from the floor, Professor Boulding made the following remark which we think is worthy of inclusion.]

What do I think of Marshall McLuhan? I should like to refer you to my review article in the *Canadian Journal of Economics and Political Science*.[1] I think McLuhan is the finest piece of mod-

[1] Kenneth E. Boulding. The Medium and the Message. Review of Marshall McLuhan, The Gutenberg Galaxy, and Understanding Media. *Can. Jour. of Econ. and Pol. Sci.* 31:2 (May 1965) pp. 268–73.

ern poetry since T. S. Eliot, and I am delighted with it. I think, however, almost every detail is wrong even though the whole spirit of it is right. I think he is right in saying that the medium is often much more important than the message. I think he goes a little too far, however, in neglecting the fact that occasionally people have something to say. I feel a bit the same way about information theory. This is absolutely wonderful for Bell Telephone but a theory which makes no distinction whatever between the conversation of a teen-ager and that of a president is a little unrealistic.

✹ ·

Trends in Service Sector Employment

✹

EDGAR WEINBERG

LABORSAVING TECHNOLOGY IS OFTEN REGARDED AS THE SOLE FORCE shaping future employment trends. Some social commentators anticipate the eventual "silent conquest" of the economy by "cybernation" and predict widespread displacement of labor. These dire forecasts are journalistically provocative, but they present an oversimplified view of reality. For one thing, they fail to take account of prospects for expanding employment opportunities in the service sector. Technological advances enable farms and factories to produce an increasing abundance of material goods with a declining proportion of the labor force; the proportion engaged as sales clerks, insurance agents, bank tellers, teachers, musicians, nurses, and other service workers, in jobs which are not easily standardized or mechanized, tends to grow. Furthermore, as average income rises, expenditures for labor-intensive services such as recreation and education tend to rise relatively faster than those for goods. This transformation from a goods-producing to a service economy has significant implications for human resource development.

EDGAR WEINBERG is Chief of the Division of Technological Studies, U.S. Bureau of Labor Statistics, Washington, D.C.

The growth of service employment has been a major factor in the postwar economy. It accounted for nearly 90 percent of the net growth in total employment since 1947. Employment in the service industries surpassed that in the goods-producing industries about ten years ago. Today about 41 million persons or over 60 percent of all workers are employed in service industries. This figure includes employment in transportation, communication, public utilities, trade, finance, insurance and real estate, business and personal services, and government.

Although detailed information is available on the type and range of manufacturing activity, we are only dimly aware of the enormous extent of some service activities. About 1.5 million persons, for example, are employed by auto retail dealers and service stations—about 600,000 more than by the automobile industry itself. Food stores employ about 1.5 million—more than all the food manufacturing plants combined.

The trend toward services has been particularly marked since the end of World War II, but a gradual upward movement was discernible several decades ago. A few economists recognized the importance of this tendency in the 1930's. Colin Clark and Allan G. Fisher, two Australians, then predicted the dominance of service industries as a third stage in the evolution of an industrial society, the first being the dominance of primary industries such as agriculture; the second, the rise of manufacturing which compensated for the decline of farming. They projected the American economy as the prototype of Western society of the future.

What is the outlook for the service sector over the next decade? Will past growth trends continue? According to projections prepared in the Bureau of Labor Statistics, employment in services over the next ten years will continue to grow at a much higher rate than that for goods-producing industries. By 1975 employment in services will reach a level of over 50 million persons or close to 40 percent more than in 1965. Employment in goods-producing industries (exclusive of agriculture) will be only about 17 percent higher. Agriculture will continue to decline. Nearly two out of three workers will be employed in services industries.

The structure of service employment, however, is changing as the total increases. Services comprise a heterogeneous group of industries, each subject to different technical and economic influences. Automation will have a significant impact on some industries, less on others. Changing consumption patterns, population growth, and government policies also affect the outlook.

Transportation, communication, and public utilities, a technically advanced sector, provide the auxiliary services for other productive activities and are closely related to the goods sector. Technological changes in these industries are extensive and productivity growth is rapid. The outlook for 1975 is for a moderate increase in employment for this group as a whole, but widely different trends are expected within the group. Railroad employment will probably continue to decline while air transportation and trucking may increase substantially as in the past. Little or no change in employment requirements is projected for communication and public utilities.

The growth of jobs in trade, which employs over 12 million persons or close to one-third of total service employment, will be moderate. By 1975 employment will be only about one-third higher than in 1965. Organizational changes, such as the spread of self-service in discount stores, rather than computer technology will have an important impact. Some consumers preferring personal contact to the serve-yourself method, however, may be a constraining factor on the spread of such changes.

Automation will have a more significant impact in the insurance industry which employs over one million persons. A Bureau of Labor Statistics study *(Impact of Office Automation in the Insurance Industry,* Bulletin 1468) recently reported that insurance companies with 80 percent of the industry's total office employment used computers. Employment in these companies grew at a much slower rate after the introduction of computers. So far, predictions of mass layoffs of clerks because of electronic data processing have not been borne out. Management's use of turnover and planning generally has minimized the impact of these changes. Only a relatively small increase in jobs, however, is anticipated by 1975. Office automation, according to this study, sharply reduces the demand for routine clerical employees and increases requirements for sales and professional employees. The industry, consequently, may no longer be an important source, as it has been in the past, of job opportunities for high school girls looking for their first job.

Employment prospects are more favorable in the banking industry which employs over 800,000 persons. An electronic revolution, however, is occurring in banks. Most of the large banks and a good proportion of the others now use computers to process the mounting volume of bank checks. Besides automation of paper work, bank customer services, including such nonfinancial services as preparing payrolls for business firms and billing services for doctors, have been greatly expanded and diversified. Despite the trend toward automation, a substantial rise in employment is expected but at a slower rate than in the past. The automated bank of the future will need more trained supervisory personnel, systems analysts, and programmers but relatively fewer bookkeepers and routine clerks. Eventually the computer may make possible the checkless economy—retail transactions will be recorded at the bank's computer by means of data transmission equipment, and the computer will automatically credit the store's account and debit the customer's.

The slowdown in the growth of employment in insurance and banking facilitates changes in the structure of service employment. It permits industries which are less affected by automation to expand employment to meet the heavy demand for services. This group of labor-intensive industries includes business services of all kinds—real estate agencies, medical and health services, private educational institutions, hotels and motels, laundries and repair services, theaters and movies, and government. These industries are expected to be among the fastest growing during the coming decade as they were in the postwar period.

Advances in computers and data communication in the next decade may even result in further proliferation of new types of services. One which is not yet existent but said to be about to bloom is the "data utility" field. Technology already enables several people to use a computer simultaneously. Eventually small and medium-sized businesses will be able to plug in for data processing services as they now do for electricity. Another potential service is the "inquiry industry" which John Diebold calls the "publishing field of the future." This will allow the sale of proprietary data over a communication system in answer to a query placed by a customer. The possibilities are unlimited, practically any information can be provided. These examples illustrate the tendency of technology (often overlooked) to make feasible the production of goods and services never before available.

Expansion of employment in the nonprofit services—i.e., health, education, and government—constitutes one of the unique features of recent economic growth in the United States. These sectors of the economy play a strategic role in improving the quality of American life. Moreover, feedback from these services, in the form of trained professional and technical manpower, contributes to quickening technological advances in other sectors of the economy.

In medical and health services, a substantial employment expansion has taken place over the past decade as medical science has advanced and organizational innovations (such as hospital insurance) for making these services widely available have been introduced. But demand for medical services continues to grow rapidly, and by 1975 a 50 percent increase over the 2 million now employed in private hospitals and medical facilities will be needed. Shortages of highly trained persons, now one of the most critical aspects of the health problem, will not be relieved significantly by technological developments. Computers, automatic laboratory equipment, and developments in hospital supply will, however, affect the need for different groups of workers. Many new occupations and specialties are emerging, such as computer specialists, inhalation therapists, prosthetics technicians, and medical electronic engineers. A National Advisory Commission on Health Manpower and the Departments of Labor and of Health, Education and Welfare are making a concerted effort to meet the manpower needs of this vital industry.

One more service industry must be considered: government. Over 10 million persons are employed by government—three-fourths by state and local governments and the rest by the federal government. By 1975 the total may rise by 50 percent, mostly at the state and local levels. Besides seeking improvements in the traditional functions of security, justice, and regulation, communities increasingly look to government to provide a more attractive physical environment, to broaden economic opportunities, and to reduce poverty. The public school system, which employs more than half of the over 8 million state and local government workers, is doing more than just providing schooling for children and teen-agers. It also is becoming an increasingly complex system of services for adults, the unemployed, and the disadvantaged.

Federal government employment has undergone a remarkable transformation in the past generation. Depression, war, and international competition have expanded government activities. At the same time, the introduction of electronic computer systems has limited the growth of routine jobs. In place of an army of clerks, the federal government now seeks highly educated persons to staff complex programs in space technology, oceanography, environmental pollution, education, social work, and urban development.

What are the social implications of these trends? Secretary of Labor Willard Wirtz recently criticized the notion that the individual exists to supply the economic system with what it needs, instead of the other way around. So long as employment is considered a satisfactory condition in its traditional sense—as covering any paid activity, regardless of its terms and conditions or the extent to which it uses the individual's potential or provides him with satisfaction—that term is insufficient for the purposes of advancing a human resources development program beyond its minimal essentials.

In this context we can look beyond the words "manpower requirements" to see if the trend toward services will meet more fully the individual worker's needs. Five points are noteworthy.

First, the growth of services opens up opportunities for highly trained employees. The services tend to employ a greater proportion of technical and professional workers than the goods industries, and the average level of education of employees in service industries is somewhat higher. This does not mean that opportunities for people with modest skills and education no longer exist. Indeed, many government job development projects in the past few years have demonstrated the feasibility of training such persons for positions in service industries as aides to more highly educated professional and technical workers.

Second, services offer some possibilities for more personalized work and some relief from repetitive, machine-paced jobs of mass production industries. This could reverse the long-term trend toward alienating the craftsman from his work that came with mechanization and the assembly line. Not tied to the rhythm of a machine, the service worker has more scope for variety and change in his work than the factory worker.

Third, the growth of service industries creates employment opportunities for women who comprise an increasing proportion of the labor force. Work in offices, stores, and other services is usually physically light. Part-time jobs, which are especially suitable for married women with some household responsibilities, are more prevalent in the service industries.

Fourth, employment in service industries appears to be more stable than in goods industries. Unemployment rates are lower and seasonal fluctuations in employment are probably fewer. On the other hand, many service workers have low wages, long hours, and a limited range of fringe benefits. These substandard conditions reflect partly the lack of unionization among service workers and their exclusion from the protection of minimum wage legislation.

Finally, the growth of service industries could open up opportunities for nonwhite workers who make up a disproportionate part of the unemployed. A proportion of this group is concentrated in the less skilled occupations and in industries which are not expected to grow as rapidly as others. If nonwhites do not gain access to white-collar and skilled jobs in the service industries at a faster rate than they have in recent years, they will continue to have more serious unemployment problems than their white fellow citizens. The complex problem of improving educational opportunities, of assuring equal employment practices and attitudes, and of providing motivation for achievement of the disadvantaged worker constitutes one of the major challenges to those engaged in human resource development.

✹

Trends Related to Agricultural Employment

✹

EBER ELDRIDGE

THE TERM "AGRICULTURAL" EMPLOYMENT IS SOMETIMES USED TO mean farm-related employment and all agri-business economic activity. In this chapter agricultural employment is defined as the agricultural census defines it: those employed actively in farm operation.

Although there are some relatively new data about agricultural employment trends, the conclusions cannot be considered new, different, or exciting. Agricultural projections made 15 to 20 years ago by many economists were so accurate that the latest census information merely confirms the projections.

Farm employment is closely related to the number of farms—particularly in Iowa—because of the family farm system dominant in Midwest agriculture. Contrary to many other industries, farm employment appears to have an inverse relationship to farm ouput: fewer farmers produce more.

Since World War II, most previous agricultural trends have accelerated. It has been profitable for a farmer to increase capital in relation to his labor. Capital has replaced some existing labor. More land, more equipment, more technology is applied to each

EBER ELDRIDGE is Professor of Economics at Iowa State University, Ames, Iowa.

Fig. 6.1. Decreases of 7 percent or more in farm numbers in Iowa counties, 1945–64.

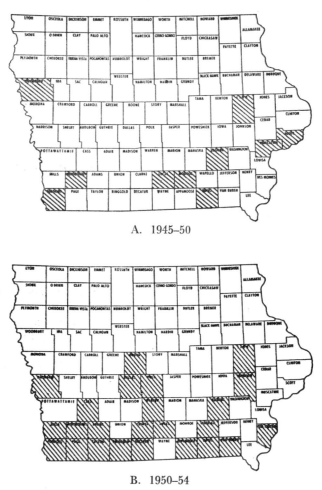

A. 1945–50

B. 1950–54

farm job and it is *profitable* to make this change. The profitability of replacing labor with capital is the primary force behind many of the agricultural trends.

DECREASES IN FARM NUMBERS

Obviously, as farmers enlarge and consolidate farms, the quality of the job might be improved, but the number of farm jobs de-

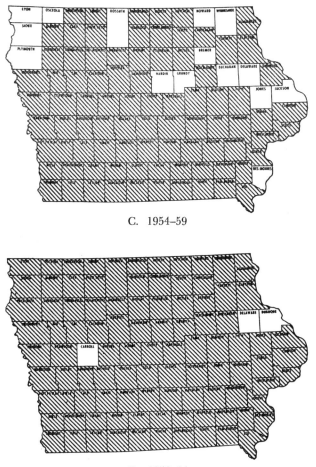

C. 1954–59

D. 1959–64

creases. Figure 6.1 relates to the change in number of farms. As you look at these maps, keep in mind the close relationship between number of farms and farm employment. Each shows the counties which have had greater than 7 percent decrease in numbers in four five-year periods.

Counties in southern Iowa—where farms are generally smaller and the capital-labor ratio in agriculture has been relatively lower—

were the first to feel the economic pressures (Fig. 6.1A). Soon after World War II, the southern Iowa counties having a large number of small farms were the first to start combining farms.

Large-city counties also had a significant decrease in farm numbers between 1945 and 1950. Sioux City, Cedar Rapids, and Davenport show their influence in the farm change. One of the strong forces in changing farm employment is the opportunity to get a nonfarm job. Availability of nonfarm jobs in the Iowa cities has been a significant factor in facilitating farm adjustment. Some farmers leave farm work and take off-farm jobs when they are within a reasonable distance from home. Consequently, counties offering a chance for nonfarm employment are also counties showing a rapid decrease in farm numbers.

Figure 6.1B shows that in the next five-year period the economic pressures increased and the reaction to these pressures increased. Again, the same two observations can be made. Southern counties with their small farms felt the economic pressures first. But the economic pressures gradually spread northward. In addition, other metropolitan counties started facilitating change, including Des Moines, Iowa City, Ottumwa, and Burlington. These population centers offered opportunities for nonfarm jobs.

The economic pressures had spread over most of Iowa by 1959 (Fig. 6.1C). There were a few holdouts in the northwest and in the northeast. Figure 6.1D completes the picture; it shows that in 1965 all areas in Iowa were subject to the economic forces causing farmers to increase their capital-labor ratio and decrease the number of farm jobs.

DECLINE ACCELERATING

Something related to this trend that is not generally recognized is illustrated in Table 6.1: The decreases in farm numbers and farm employment are taking place at an increasing rate. The latest census information shows an increasing percentage rate of decrease. Table 6.1 shows that the first five-year period had a 2.8 percent farm decrease, the second five-year period 5 percent, the third period

TABLE 6.1

CHANGE IN NUMBERS OF IOWA FARMS BY FIVE-YEAR PERIODS, 1945–65

Year	Number Change	Percent Change
1945–50	— 5,795	— 2.8
1950–54	—10,226	— 5.0
1954–59	—18,226	— 9.4
1959–64	—16,797	—11.8

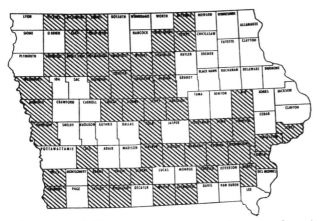

Fig. 6.2. Decreases of 12 percent or more in farm numbers in Iowa counties, 1959–65.

9.4 percent, and the most recent five-year period 11.8 percent. The present rate of change represents the loss of over 30,000 jobs in Iowa in a ten-year period. The rate of change continues to gain momentum, according to the latest information available.

Note that the absolute number change was not as great in the last five-year period as in 1954–59. Although the absolute number of farm consolidations is decreasing, the percentage change is increasing.

In order to determine where the most rapid change in farm numbers is taking place, an arbitrary figure of 12 percent decrease was selected (Fig. 6.2). This map shows that the high rate of decline has spread over most of the state. Except for a few counties in northeast Iowa (a dairy area) there seems to be no area of the state untouched by rapid change in farm employment. Keep in mind that the counties shaded in Figure 6.2 represent a decrease in farm numbers and farm employment of one-fourth in ten years—one out of every four farms is being consolidated in a ten-year period if the present rate continues through 1969.

There has been some speculation that the counties with the most rapid change in farm numbers have reached their peak of decline and are now tapering off. Figure 6.3 shows the counties which had a lower rate of change in the latest five-year period than in the previous period. There are 23 counties in this category.

The counties shaded have a rapid rate of change, but in these counties there is some indication that in the last five years, the

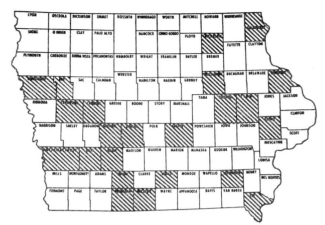

Fig. 6.3. Counties with a decreasing rate of change in farm numbers, 1959–64.

rate of change has stabilized. This does *not* mean that farm consolidation has ceased. It does *not* mean that the rapid rate of change will not continue in the future. It only means that in these counties, the rate of change did not become more severe in the last five-year period than in the preceding five-year period.

Due to the belief about a "stable rate of change," it has been suggested that in the future, southern Iowa will not undergo as severe an adjustment period as in the past.

There is no evidence to support this popular conclusion. Gross sales per farm are correlated with the capital-labor ratio. The larger the capital-labor ratio, the greater the gross sales per farm, in general. Figure 6.4 shows the average gross sales per farm for each county. Levels of sales are highest in northern Iowa and lowest in southern Iowa. The average for some of the northern counties is three to four times that of the average of some of the southern counties.

Even though the southern counties started consolidating farms earlier and have reached a more rapid rate of consolidation, the capital-labor ratio in southern Iowa is still low relative to the northern part of the state. Consequently the pressures for farm consolidation are still greater in southern Iowa relative to northern Iowa.

Economic pressures will continue consolidation in southern Iowa, but there is reason to believe that the adjustment in the future may be more rapid in northern than in southern Iowa. In

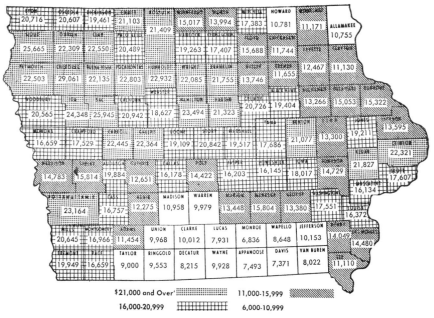

Fig. 6.4. Average gross sales per farm in Iowa counties, 1964.

Monroe County, in southern Iowa, 90 percent of the farms are owner-operated. In Osceola County, in northern Iowa, 50 percent of the farms are owner-operated. Southern Iowa counties typically have a high percentage of owner operation, northern Iowa counties typically a lower percentage.

An owner-operated farm is less flexible in terms of adjustment. In northern Iowa where approximately half the farms have leases reconsidered each year, the opportunities to change, to adjust, and to consolidate are much greater than in southern Iowa where the owner-operator pattern gives more rigidity.

MORE SALES PER FARM

Total gross sales from farm sources in Iowa increased in the last ten years by over 40 percent. Average gross sales per farm increased even more (Fig. 6.5). Gross sales of $20,000 are associated with net incomes of $6,000 to $8,000. Northwestern Iowa counties have the highest proportion of farms with gross sales of $20,000 or more. These farms are numerous all along the western Iowa border. The number of farms in this category increased 35 percent for the

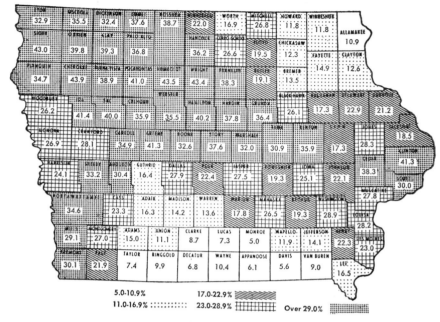

Fig. 6.5. Percent of farms with gross sales exceeding $20,000 in Iowa counties, 1964.

state between 1959 and 1964. Cherokee County in northwestern Iowa had the greatest proportion of these farms of any county in Iowa in 1964, about 44 percent.

SUMMARY OF MAJOR TRENDS

Table 6.2 summarizes the major trends in agriculture in Iowa. The data are for the "typical" cash grain Corn Belt farm. Typical is defined as being the most common. Although these are not average data, they do illustrate the major trends taking place.

Size of farm is increasing. The amount of labor used on the family farm is remaining about constant, with a general decrease in hired labor. Total capital invested per farm is increasing. Many typical farms have investments of over $100,000.

In this five-year period (1959–64), cash receipts went up substantially more than cash expenditures, bringing a net farm income increase of over 200 percent. This is still a big increase, even when inflation is considered. Returns per hour associated with this income are up more than 400 percent. Farm production and pro-

TABLE 6.2

TYPICAL CORN BELT CASH GRAIN FARMS

	1957–59 Average	1963	Percent Change
Land in farm (acres)	237	289	+ 21.9
Cropland	196	246	+ 25.5
Total labor (hours)	3,290	3,340	+ 01.5
Family	2,930	3,010	+ 02.7
Hired	360	330	− 08.3
Total capital	$100,090	$137,020	+ 36.9
Total cash receipts	13,558	24,076	+ 77.6
Total cash expenditures	7,607	10,840	+ 42.5
Net farm income	6,706	14,311	+213.4
(1947–49 dollars)	5,717	11,730	+205.1
Return per hour	.48	2.18	+454.1
Net farm production	100	162	+ 62
Production per hour labor	100	160	+ 60
Prices received	100	105	+ 05

Source: USDA Agr. Inf. Bul. No. 230, June 1964.

duction per hour of labor are both up substantially, while prices received have increased but little. Table 6.2 illustrates some of the major changes, but it also points out some of the reasons for the major changes—economic motivation associated with increased returns.

DOES FARM CONSOLIDATION PAY?

The question is frequently asked: "Does farm consolidation really pay?" Table 6.3 shows that a 560-acre farm has tremendous cost advantages over a 160-acre farm. The larger the farm, the less the expense per acre. Consequently the larger farmer is operating at a distinct competitive advantage over the smaller operator. Attempting to get the advantages of lower production costs is a primary motivation behind farm consolidation.

If a farmer is unable to accumulate sufficient capital or to rent a farm large enough to provide him the competitive cost advantages

TABLE 6.3

EXPENSES PER ACRE BY SIZE OF FARM, 1965 IOWA FARM BUSINESS RECORDS

Farm Size	Expense
acres	dollars
160	90.99
240	79.11
320	67.23
440	63.07
560	55.59
Larger	?

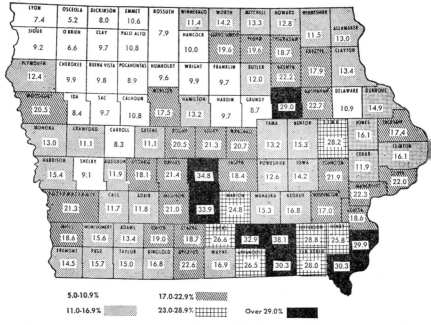

Fig. 6.6. Percent of farmers working off their farms 100 days or more in
Iowa counties, 1964.

of larger operation, he sometimes turns to another alternative. If
he is within driving distance of a nonfarm job, he will frequently
supplement his income from the small farm operation with the
off-farm job. There are some counties where nearly one-third of
the farmers are working in nonfarm jobs. Figure 6.6 shows that
where this occurs, there is also substantial nonfarm economic activity which provides opportunities for nonfarm employment, such
as near Des Moines, Waterloo, Ottumwa, and Burlington. Farmers
will often drive 55 to 60 miles one way to work.

In spite of the high rate of consolidation in the past and the
substantial degree of consolidation that has already taken place,
there is still room for improvement in the capital-labor ratio in the
farming industry in Iowa. Figure 6.7 shows the percent of farms
in each county with gross sales under $10,000 in 1964. Ten thou-
sand dollars gross sales is associated with $3,000 net income. This
approaches the poverty level, according to the Office of Economic
Opportunity.

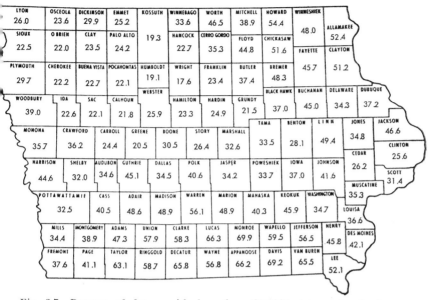

Fig. 6.7. Percent of farms with less than $10,000 gross sales in Iowa counties, 1964.

In southern Iowa, many counties had over half the farms near the poverty income level in 1964. In the northern larger-farm area, one-fourth to one-third of the farms were in this category. Figure 6.7 reminds us that, although tremendous improvement has been made in substituting capital for labor in the farming industry in Iowa, there are still weaknesses in the structure. As farmers attempt to strengthen their competitive position in Iowa agriculture, farm consolidation will continue.

FUTURE TRENDS

We have examined past trends and the present situation. Before we can relate these trends to farm employment in the future, we must anticipate future trends. Earl Heady, Iowa State University economist, has this to say about the future of agriculture:

> The process of replacing labor with capital will occur more rapidly in the future. The following reasons might be given: (1) The numerous national programs aimed at reducing economic disadvantages and aimed toward improved education and outlook. (2) The

growing intensity and effectiveness of communication and mobility among regional and economic sectors. (3) The fact that we know more about the process of substituting capital for labor. (4) The fact that competition within the farm industry is gathering momentum as agricultural resources move into the hands of stronger managers.[1]

In addition, Dr. Heady says, "An investment of $200,000 per farm may well define the lower bounds for the successful commercial farm by 1980."[2] Dr. Heady's projections include the following: The number of farms in the nation will decline from 3.2 million to 1.5 million between 1960 and 1980. Farm employment will decline from 6 million persons in 1960 to 3.5 million in 1980. He says it is possible that we might have only 2.5 million farm workers by 1980. The lower figure receives support from a Department of Labor publication[3] which said that between 1960 and 1964, farm employment declined from 6 million to 4.8 million.

These conclusions can be drawn about the farming industry: (1) The rate of change is rapid and will continue. (2) The number of farm jobs will decrease more in the next ten years than in the last ten. (3) Total income from farming is up. (4) As the capital-labor ratio improves, individual farm income will improve. (5) The farming industry is getting structurally stronger and is contributing to economic growth. (6) There are still many small farms with low incomes in the farming industry.

In terms of job opportunities we can say: There are many good jobs in farming if the individual has enough capital to combine with his labor to make his labor sufficiently productive. If the individual does not have capital to make his operation competitive, his opportunities in the farming industry will be reduced.

WHO FARMS?

These are statements about the farming industry in general. The basic question has not been answered: Which kind of farm job, good or bad, does the new entrant have when he starts farming? Kaldor and Jetton[4] found that in 1960 in Iowa, there were 2,522 new entrants. Of these, 89 percent were beginning farmers. The rate of entry was 1.65 percent, the rate of withdrawal from

---

[1] Farm Policy Forum, Vol. 18, No. 3, 1965–66.

[2] Paper prepared for the Southwest Agricultural Forum, Jan. 19, 1967, Tulsa, Okla., p. 10.

[3] Trends in Farm Employment and Training Needs, Reprint No. 9, Aug. 1966. U.S. Department of Labor, Washington, D.C.

[4] Research Bulletin 546, Aug. 1966, Agr. Exp. Sta., Iowa State University.

agriculture was 3.1 percent, giving an annual rate of decline of 1.5 percent.

At the 1960 rate of decline, accepted projections for 1980 will not be reached. The entry rate would have to decline or the withdrawal rate increase before the 1980 projections could be reached.

The typical Iowa farm entrant in 1960 was 25 years old and had lived on a farm before entering farming. Two-thirds were high school graduates, 5 percent had completed college, and 43 percent had taken vocational training.

It appears that the old idea of climbing the agricultural ladder—where a boy lived on a farm, hired out as a farmhand, accumulated some money, bought a cow, and then rented a farm—is no longer true, if it ever were. Seventy-eight percent of the Iowa entrants in 1960 had held a full-time nonfarm job before entering farming.

The average land base was 165 acres. This is a relatively small base and places the new entrant at a great competitive disadvantage with the established farmer.

Some more information about new entrants into farming: Two-thirds performed nonfarm work while farming. Seventy-nine percent had worked on other farms and one-fifth of the wives held nonfarm jobs. The average family income was $6,180 annually, 51 percent of which came from farming.

Although there were some who felt satisfied with their farming experience, 34 percent said rewards were less than expected, and 30 percent said that they had thought about quitting because of low income.

SUMMARY

The study of the farm entrants reaffirms the conclusion that there are good opportunities in farming if you have a good capital-labor ratio. But the number of farm jobs will continue to decline rapidly. Some beginning farmers have enough capital to operate an economic unit. However, some go on relatively small farms where they face exceedingly tough competition.

The data associated with the farm employment trends tend to support the major point of this chapter—although there are good opportunities in farming, millions of farm people and millions of farm youth will need training, education, and preparation for a nonfarm way of life.

✳

Trends and Projections
of Manufacturing Employment in Iowa

✳

GENE FUTRELL

PAST EMPLOYMENT IN MANUFACTURING INDUSTRIES IN IOWA AS WELL as total employment has been strongly influenced by the major role of agriculture in the economy of the state. A natural endowment of fertile soil plus climatic conditions favorable for grain production has provided distinct comparative advantages in the production of feed grains and livestock. At the same time, a general lack of mineral resources has limited the opportunity for development of other basic industries. As a result, manufacturing employment has historically accounted for a relatively small proportion of total employment in the state.

Iowa's role as a leading agricultural producing state appears certain to continue. But technological advances in agriculture have brought tremendous gains in productivity per farm worker. Iowa agriculture has become less labor-intensive and increasingly capital-intensive in economic character. The number of people employed in agricultural production has dropped sharply and will

GENE FUTRELL is Associate Professor of Economics at Iowa State University, Ames, Iowa.

continue to trend down. This has released labor resources for non-agricultural occupations, including those in manufacturing industries.

Over the years a sizable part of the labor supply shifted out of agriculture, and many of the new entrants to the Iowa labor force have been "exported" to other states because nonagricultural employment opportunities in Iowa were not available in sufficient number. Many future entrants to Iowa's nonagricultural labor force, through population growth and further shifts of labor from agriculture, will likewise be attracted to out-of-state employment unless employment opportunities in manufacturing and other non-agricultural industries expand accordingly.

Manufacturing Employment

Despite the past outmigration of labor, there have been substantial gains in manufacturing and other types of nonagricultural employment in Iowa. And the relative importance of these industries and the related occupational specialties has greatly increased. In broad terms this can be illustrated by the change in relative value of agricultural and industrial output in the state. The value of Iowa's industrial output in 1965 was three times as great as the state's agricultural output. Prior to 1950 the value of agricultural production exceeded that of industrial production.

Specifically, manufacturing employment in Iowa doubled from 1940 to 1965, increasing from 95,600 to 190,800. This was a more rapid rate of increase than the national gain of 64 percent in manufacturing employment during the same period, and it compared with an increase of 24 percent in total employment in Iowa from 1940 to 1955. During the same period the number of persons employed in agricultural production in Iowa declined by 38 percent. The biggest gain in manufacturing employment occurred between 1940 and 1950 (up 62 percent). This was followed by a 14 percent increase from 1950 to 1960 and a further gain of 8 percent from 1960 to 1965. Manufacturing employment accounted for only 11 percent of total employment in Iowa in 1940. Although still relatively small, the proportion increased to 18 percent by 1965. These broad changes in employment distribution in Iowa are shown in more detail in Tables 7.1 and 7.2.

Most of the increase in manufacturing employment in Iowa during recent years has been in durable goods industries (Table 7.3). This has occurred despite the relative importance of agricultural processing industries in the state. Total employment in durable goods manufacturing increased from 75,300 in 1950 to 106,800

TABLE 7.1

IOWA EMPLOYMENT AND EMPLOYMENT DISTRIBUTION BY SELECTED GROUPINGS

	1940		1950		1960		1965	
	Number Employed	Per cent	Number Employed	Per cent	Number Employed	Per cent	Number Employed	Per cent
	thousands		*thousands*		*thousands*		*thousands*	
Agriculture }*	308.8	35.7	285.3	28.4	210.2	20.6	190.0[1]	17.7[1]
Nonagriculture	554.0	64.3	717.8	71.6	810.5	79.4	881.7[2]	82.3[2]
Manufacturing[3]	95.6	11.2	154.4	15.4	176.6	17.3	190.8	17.8
Nonmanufacturing[4]	347.7	40.3	461.8	46.1	507.3	49.7	559.7	52.3
Other[5]	110.7	12.8	101.6	10.1	126.6	12.4	131.2[1]	12.2[2]
* Total	862.8	100.0	1,003.1	100.0	1,020.7	100.0	1,071.7[2]	100.0

[1] Estimated.
[2] Partly estimated.
[3] Excludes proprietors and self-employed.
[4] Excludes proprietors, self-employed, domestic workers, and armed forces.
[5] Proprietors, self-employed, domestic workers, and armed forces.

Source: Employment and Earnings Statistics for States and Areas, 1939–1965, Bul. No. 1370-3, BLS, USDL, June 1966; and Growth Patterns in Employment by County, 1940–1950 and 1950–1960 (Volume 4, Plains), Office of Business Economics, USDC, 1965.

TABLE 7.2

CHANGE IN EMPLOYMENT IN IOWA BY SELECTED GROUPINGS AND TIME PERIODS

	Employment 1940	Change in Employment				
		1940–65	1940–65	1940–50	1950–60	1960–65
	thousands	thousands	percent	percent	percent	percent
Agriculture *	308.7	−118.7	− 38	− 8	−26	−10[1]
Nonagricultural ∫	554.0	+327.7	+ 59	+30	+13	+ 9
Manufacturing[2]	95.6	+ 95.2	+100	+62	+14	+ 8
Nonmanufacturing[3]	347.7	+212.0	+ 61	+33	+10	+10
Other[4]	110.7	+ 20.5	+ 19	− 8	+25	+ 4
* Total	862.8	+208.9	+ 24	+16	+ 2	+ 5[1]

[1] Estimated.
[2] Excludes proprietors and self-employed.
[3] Excludes proprietors, self-employed, domestic workers, and armed forces.
[4] Proprietors, self-employed, domestic workers, and armed forces.

Source: Employment and Earnings Statistics for States and Areas, 1939–65, Bul. No. 1370-3, BLS, USDL, June 1966; and Growth Patterns in Employment by County, 1940–1950 and 1950–1960 (Volume 4, Plains), Office of Business Economics, USDC, 1965.

TABLE 7.3

IOWA MANUFACTURING EMPLOYMENT

	Number Employed			Percent Change	
	1950	1960	1965	1950–60	1960–65
	thousands	thousands	thousands		
All manufacturing[1]	154.4	176.6	190.8	+14	+ 8
Durable goods	75.3	94.1	106.8	+25	+13
Lumber & furniture	7.9	7.5	6.4	− 5	−15
Stone, clay, & glass	5.6	6.8	6.1	+21	−10
Primary metals	4.8	6.4	7.8	+33	+22
Fabricated metal products	8.5	9.6	10.8	+13	+13
Machinery (excl. elec.)	29.4	33.6	41.1	+14	+22
Farm mach. & equip.	18.7	21.5	26.0	+15	+21
Constr. & mining mach.	4.6	5.0	6.2	+ 9	+24
Electrical machinery	10.1	19.4	22.7	+92	+17
Transportation equipment	2.5	2.2	2.9	−12	+32
Other	6.5	8.6	9.0	+32	+ 5
Nondurable goods	79.1	82.5	84.0	+ 4	+ 2
Food & kindred products	54.0	53.4	51.5	− 1	− 4
Meat products	28.5	27.3	25.6	− 4	− 6
Grain products	8.0	8.8	9.3	+10	+ 6
Apparel	4.2	3.8	4.0	−10	+ 5
Printing & publishing	10.4	11.9	12.1	+14	+ 2
Chemical & allied products	4.4	5.1	6.2	+16	+22
Other	6.1	8.3	10.2	+36	+23

[1] Excludes proprietors and self-employed.
Source: Employment and Earnings Statistics for States and Areas, 1939–1965, Bul. No. 1370-3, BLS, USDL, June 1966.

in 1965—up 31,500 or 42 percent. By contrast, employment in non-durable manufacturing rose only 6 percent—from 79,100 in 1950 to 84,000 in 1965.

Within the durable goods grouping, two industries account for a large share of the manufacturing employment and have accounted for much of the employment increase in recent years. These are farm machinery and equipment, with 26,000 manufacturing employees in 1965 (14 percent of total manufacturing employment) and electrical machinery, with 22,700 employees in 1965 (12 percent). These two industries accounted for over half of the total increase in manufacturing employment in Iowa from 1950 to 1965. Other major durable goods industries that employed 6,000 or more persons in Iowa in 1965 included fabricated metal products, primary metals, lumber and furniture, construction machinery, and stone, glass, and clay.

In the nondurable goods classification, food and kindred products account for a major share of the manufacturing employment in Iowa. This broad industry grouping is also the largest single source of manufacturing employment in the state. It includes such important subclassifications as meat packing, dairy processing and manufacturing, manufactured feeds, cereals, bakery products, soybean processing, and corn processing. Despite its substantial role in total manufacturing employment in the state, the actual number of employees in food and kindred product industries has declined slightly during recent years.

The largest single industry in the food and kindred products grouping is meat packing. The number of meat packing employees in 1965 totaled 25,600 compared with 28,500 in 1950. The grain-mill products industry showed a moderate employment gain in the same period, increasing from 8,000 to 9,300.

The printing and publishing industry represents the other major source of nondurable manufacturing employment in Iowa. Numerous other industries account for the balance of the manufacturing employment in nondurables, with chemical and allied products and apparel among the more important. The small gain in nondurable goods manufacturing employment between 1950 and 1965 occurred primarily in chemical and allied products, grain-mill products, and several smaller industries.

AGRICULTURALLY RELATED EMPLOYMENT

The relative importance of Iowa's agricultural producing industry has provided a strong economic base for the development of a sizable manufacturing industry in food and related products. Similarly it has provided the basis for many manufacturing, distribution, and service activities on the input or farm supply side of agricultural production. Employment trends in the food and kindred product industries of the state have already been described, as have the trends in employment in farm machinery manufacturing. These two groupings account for a major part of the manufacturing employment that can be considered as agriculturally related.

It is difficult to identify all of the employment in Iowa that is agriculturally related. On the input side, it encompasses the manufacture of commercial feeds, agricultural chemicals, fertilizers, machinery and equipment, building materials, and many other items. It also includes a wide range of service activities such as feed mixing and distribution, credit, veterinary services, fuel and petroleum needs, electrical power, machinery repair, equipment, and other farm supply retailing. On the distribution side, employment in firms purchasing and handling farm products is included.

A partial listing of employment in the more obvious agriculturally related manufacturing industries and businesses is shown in Table 7.4.[1] Although an incomplete summation of agriculturally related employment, it still represents 17 percent of all nonagricultural employment in Iowa in 1964. The employment represented by these industries is not related solely to Iowa agriculture. This is especially true of the large farm machinery industry which is a sizable exporter to other states and countries.

FUTURE EMPLOYMENT PROSPECTS IN MANUFACTURING

The foregoing has been a somewhat cursory look at manufacturing employment trends in Iowa during the past 15 to 25 years. In looking ahead, I have relied largely upon the work of several people who have developed specific projections of future manufacturing employment and of needs in specific occupational specialties.[2] In addition, I have added several more general observations on possible trends during the next several years.

Projections to 1970 by Bognanno and Hagen place total employment in Iowa at 1,116,496 compared with 1,020,700 in 1960. That would be a gain of nearly 100,000 or a little over 9 percent.[3]

---

[1] The manufacturing data in Table 7.4 are from a different source than those shown in Table 7.3 and are therefore not completely comparable.

[2] M. F. Bognanno and V. C. Hagen, "Principal Employment Changes in Iowa From 1940 to 1960, With Projections to 1970," *Iowa Business Digest*, Vol. 37, No. 5, Bureau of Business and Economic Research, University of Iowa, May 1966; E. B. Jakubauskas, *Job Opportunities for Iowa's Youth*, Special Report No. 46, Iowa State University, Feb. 1966.

[3] Bognanno and Hagen, *op. cit.*

TABLE 7.4

Employment in Selected Agriculturally Related Industries in Iowa[1]

	Number Employed			Number of Units		
	1951	1959	1964	1951	1959	1964
Manufacturing:						
Food & kindred products	47,811	53,047	47,122	1,051	1,065	855
Meat packing plants	27,532	25,244	22,174	127	63	67
Poultry processing plants	. . .	1,608	1,417	. . .	31	32
Dairy products	4,152	6,340	5,649	393	439	319
Canning, preserving, & freezing	951	1,384	1,318	41	27	27
Grain mill products	4,803	8,465	7,843	154	170	186
Prepared feeds	. . .	3,980	3,830	. . .	153	168
Bakery products	. . .	. . .	3,665	. . .	. . .	76
Soybean oil mills	. . .	999	920	. . .	20	18
Agricultural chemicals	. . .	536	1,000	. . .	30	41
Fertilizers	. . .	294	319	. . .	11	9
Fertilizer, mixing only	. . .	191	562	. . .	14	26
Farm machinery & equipment	. . .	22,884	22,871	. . .	117	121
Wholesale Trade:						
Farm products, raw material	. . .	6,214	5,208	. . .	1,017	888
Farm machinery & equipment	. . .	678	779	. . .	48	64
Retail Trade:						
Farm equipment dealers	. . .	4,675	4,390	. . .	1,076	913
Farm & garden supply stores	. . .	4,558	6,052	. . .	978	1,147
Services:						
Agricultural credit	. . .	. . .	81	. . .	. . .	12
Animal husbandry services	. . .	1,449	1,606	. . .	531	541
Other agricultural services	. . .	523	1,112	. . .	162	228

[1] Not complete enumeration of employment in agriculture related industries.
Source: County Business Patterns, Iowa, Bureau of the Census, USDC (1964, 1959 and 1951 issues).

All of the projected increase is in the employment of women, with a small decline in male employment. Manufacturing employment is projected to show a larger relative increase—up 30 percent from 1960 to 1970 to a total of 242,295 (Table 7.5). All job categories in manufacturing except laborers are projected to show employment gains. Largest increases are projected in professional and technical, operative and clerical workers. Smaller gains are projected for managers, proprietors, craftsmen, and foremen and service workers. Approximately four-fifths of the projected increase in manufacturing employment is for male workers. However, sizable increases in female workers in clerical and operative jobs in manufacturing industries are indicated.

Projections of manufacturing employment in Iowa to 1970 by Jakubauskas[4] indicate employment of 244,059—very close to that

[4] Jakubauskas, *op. cit.*

TABLE 7.5

Iowa Manufacturing Employment by Occupational Categories,
1950, 1960, and Projected 1970

	1950		1960		1970	
	Male	Female	Male	Female	Male	Female
Professional, technical, and kindred workers	5,478	1,011	10,378	1,354	20,589	1,859
Managers, officials, and proprietors (incl. farm)	8,302	530	10,085	530	12,467	530
Clerical, sales, and kindred workers	14,111	10,675	18,345	14,906	24,398	21,404
Craftsmen, foremen, and kindred workers	28,853	1,395	33,334	1,507	39,027	1,640
Operatives and kindred workers	47,270	15,525	60,276	20,170	78,516	26,808
Service workers	2,657	376	2,894	587	3,178	937
Laborers (incl. farm)	13,776	1,137	11,871	772	10,393	549
Total	120,447	30,649	147,183	39,826	188,568	53,727

Source: M. F. Bognanno and V. C. Hagen, "Principal Employment Changes in Iowa from 1940 to 1960, With Projections to 1970," *Iowa Business Digest*, Vol. 27, No. 5, pp. 14–15, Bureau of Business and Economic Research, University of Iowa, May 1966.

projected by Bognanno and Hagen. Further projections to 1980 are for total manufacturing employment in Iowa of 289,424, a 19 percent increase from 1970. These projections reflect fairly comparable percentage gains in manufacturing employment by both men and women.

In what industries do growth prospects for manufacturing employment appear most promising? Recent gains in manufacturing employment have been greatest in the durable goods category, especially in the production of farm machinery, electrical machinery, and certain fabricated metal products. Iowa's advantage in these areas is largely one of market orientation. The state is well located with respect to distribution of finished products where a national or broad central states regional market is involved. This advantage is especially relevant for products in which the value of the finished goods is relatively high with respect to raw material costs—and where raw materials that are shipped in are not excessively bulky.

Electronics and electrical machinery industries would appear to meet these criteria. They should also have strong growth potential on a national scale. With a sizable electronics and electrical machinery industry already established in Iowa, there should be good opportunity for further expansion. This assumes that the economic and institutional climate will be favorable enough to encourage existing companies to expand or for new firms to locate in the state. Similarly the present manufacturing base in farm machinery and equipment and in several fabricated metal product industries should provide some advantage in obtaining a share of any future national growth in these industries.

Agriculturally Related Manufacturing

Prospects appear favorable for at least moderate employment growth in several agriculturally related industries. Here the advantage is primarily one of ready access to raw materials, combined with transportation efficiencies in transporting the resulting processed items. The meat packing industry is an important example. The competitive position of Iowa in the production and feeding of cattle and hogs should at least be maintained during the next 10 to 15 years. Absolute expansion in cattle feeding is likely to be substantial while hog production is expected to show moderate growth. There is a strong trend toward production-oriented slaughter and processing of livestock products. This has been reflected in the rapid growth of new slaughtering plants in Iowa during the past few years. With livestock production expected to increase, there is a strong probability that slaughtering and processing activity will also expand. Although automation in this industry may lower labor requirements per unit, volume gains should be sufficient to bring a moderate increase in employment requirements.

While the number of livestock slaughtering plants has been increasing, the trend in most other agricultural processing industries has been in the other direction. Considerable downward adjustment in the number of processing and handling firms has occurred in the dairy and poultry industries. Size and volume of business per firm have increased while the number of manufacturing employees has declined. In the grain industry, the number of grain handling firms is expected to drop sharply during the next several years. Volume per firm and total volume of grain production and handling in Iowa are likely to increase during the next few years. However, it appears likely that any gain in employment in the industry will be slight.

Manufacturing employment related to farm supplies or inputs for agricultural production is likely to show some increase in Iowa. Agriculture is becoming increasingly commercialized. Capital inputs continue to replace labor and land resources, and individual farming operations are becoming larger and more specialized. These developments are increasing the demand for purchased inputs for the farm business, such as commercially prepared feeds, fertilizers, and agricultural chemicals. This trend is expected to continue and should provide some potential for growth of related manufacturing industries in Iowa. Along with this is the potential for expanded employment in related distribution and service industries, such as farm supply retail outlets, feed mixing and distribution, and other service activities.

Other Nondurable Goods Industries

Aside from the agriculturally related industries, moderate employment gains also appear possible in several other nondurable goods industries. Employment in the chemical, apparel, and printing and publishing industries has shown moderate gains during the past five years. These and other products requiring readily transportable raw materials which have a high value in relation to their bulk and which are oriented to broad regional or national markets are most likely to register gains in the next few years.

Other Influences on Manufacturing Employment

There are some other things in the picture that may aid Iowa's industrial growth in the years ahead. One is the substantial research at our major universities in such areas as engineering, physics, metallurgy, medicine, and atomic energy. The existence of this large research effort within the state should help to attract research-oriented industries—both research organizations per se and manufacturers. The Federal Animal Disease Laboratory at Ames is an example.

Also promoting Iowa's growth are the efforts and activities of the Iowa Development Commission in bringing locational opportunities to the attention of potential new industries, working with Iowa industries and communities in developing and promoting expansion and new development of industry, and providing financial support for research and other efforts related to the economic growth of the state.

The Center for Industrial Research and Service (CIRAS) located at Iowa State University and the Bureau of Business and Economic Research at the University of Iowa are other positive factors in the picture. Finally, the growing interest in developing the human resources of the state—as evidenced by the establishment of the Iowa State Manpower Development Council in 1965—is a strong positive force in appraising the prospects for future industrial growth in Iowa.

IMPLICATIONS

Substantial gains in manufacturing employment in Iowa during the next 10 to 15 years appear possible. However, it is by no means certain that these gains will materialize. It will depend in part upon the economic and institutional environment that prevails during the next few years within the state. The actual supply of labor as well as the productivity potential of the new additions to the labor force will be important.

Population growth in Iowa during the next ten years will be greatest in the age group of 15 to 25 years.[5] The number of people in the 25 to 65 age range is projected to decline slightly. The industrial and business world will be more demanding in the educational and vocational training requirements for employment. Providing the facilities and other resources so that the new entrants to Iowa's labor force can meet these requirements will be a major challenge to the people of this state. It will demand improved and expanded programs of general and professional education and vocational training for the new entrants to the labor force and expanded programs for training and retraining for those who lack vocational skills or require new training in order to compete for available jobs.

[5] Jon Doerflinger and Ronald Klimek, *Iowa's Population: Recent Trends and Future Prospects*, Special Report No. 47, Agr. and Home Econ. Exp. Sta., Iowa State University, May 1966.

SELECTED REFERENCES

Bognanno, M. F., and Hagen, V. C., "Principal Employment Changes in Iowa From 1940 to 1960, With Projections to 1970," *Iowa Business Digest*, Vol. 37, No. 5, Bureau of Business and Economic Research, University of Iowa, May 1966.

Doerflinger, Jon, and Klimek, Ronald, *Iowa's Population: Recent Trends and Future Propsects*, Special Report No. 47, Agr. and Home Econ. Exp. Sta., Iowa State University, May 1966.

Jakubauskas, E. B., *Job Opportunities for Iowa's Youth*, Special Report No. 46, Iowa State University, Feb. 1966.

Maki, W. C., *Projections of Iowa's Economy and People in 1974*, Special Report No. 41, Agr. and Home Econ. Exp. Sta., Iowa State University, Jan. 1965.

USDC, Office of Business Economics, *Growth Patterns in Employment by County 1940–1950 and 1950–1960* (Vol. 4, Plains), 1965.

USDC, Bureau of the Census, *County Business Patterns, Iowa* (1964, 1959, 1951 issues).

USDL, B.L.S. *Employment and Earnings Statistics for States and Areas, 1939–1965*, Bul. No. 1370-3, June 1966.

✳

The Challenge of the Manpower Crisis

✳

JOSEPH G. COLMEN

IRONICALLY THE MANPOWER CRISIS OF THE 1960's SPRINGS FROM TWO divergent sources. In a country with the best and the most comprehensive educational system in the world, there is a huge population burdened by lack of either basic or specific skills over-represented in the ranks of the unemployed. Youth, inexperienced Negro, undereducated handicapped, technologically disabled, aging—these feel most severely the brunt of poverty. At the same time, in a full economy there is paradoxically a tight labor market. The need for manpower is acute in many industries and in most areas.

This group of hard-core unemployed, those who cannot get jobs even when jobs are plentiful, is the target for many new programs designed to develop or restore their employability. We take the position that there is no such thing as unemployability if a person can learn.

The development and use of human resources has been a critical concern of every society. Human resources have provided the margin, in peace as in war, that determined whether or not a so-

JOSEPH G. COLMEN is Deputy Assistant Secretary for Education, U.S. Department of Health, Education and Welfare, Washington, D.C.

ciety survived. But as a result, the development of human resources has meant exploitation of most people most of the time.

HUMAN POTENTIAL OR EXPLOITATION

Today we are at a new junction of human history. We now have at our disposal realistic means to think of human resources in terms of human potential rather than human exploitation. The goal of human resource development should be to achieve nothing less than what Thomas Wolfe called the "hope and promise of America," that every man should become whatever he had in his manhood to let him become. Maimonides, Hebrew philosopher, charged his people to "anticipate charity by preventing poverty; assist the reduced fellow-man . . . by teaching him a trade or putting him in the way of business, so that he may earn an honest livelihood, and not be forced to the dreadful alternative of holding out his hand to charity."

Unless we can just once hitch our goal in human resource development to this ultimate pretension, we will not do all we must with the technology at hand to free people to develop to their best, to expand their choices, to release their utmost potential for growth.

WORK AGAINST ODDS

Given the will, we must still work against substantial, even staggering, odds. Even in our affluent society, a quarter of a nation exists below the poverty line. In the world, only North America and Western Europe and a few other pockets—the total still a small minority of the earth's people—constitute islands of some comfort in a sea of economic misery. Moreover, to date at least, the gap widens, as population grows faster than capital resources. If the growth rates of the past several years hold in the United States, our population will reach one billion in another hundred years. By the year 2000, the present number of 3.5 billion humans on the face of the earth will have doubled. Man does not live by bread alone, but we must give great and urgent effort to the tasks of getting him above ignorance, poverty, and toil. All of that must be secured for him individually, before we can hope realistically to develop the good life and permanent peace.

Much will depend on the success of America in becoming a pilot society in the proper development of human resources. We have the great physical power, the most highly developed technology, and the long-standing, stable, political tradition of freedom, and it will take all of these things. If we do not solve the problems, no one else will in the foreseeable future. Moreover, the magnitude of the demand upon us should give us more urgency than pride.

Yet the disparity between the skills our economy requires and the skills available in the labor force has created for us a problem of chronic unemployment.

There have been a number of myths about unemployment. Terry Sanford, former Governor of North Carolina, stated them well:

1. That our economic system will overcome the obstacles of our society in the long run.
2. That the Horatio Alger philosophy will enable anyone of character to advance.
3. That "things are just fine," or we need to do just a bit more.
4. That money will solve all our problems.

None of these applies today. For example, it is unlikely that employment among those groups where its lack is most serious will increase solely through the economic growth of our nation. Improvement for these people will come only through increasing the preparation and training of those who have been left out of the educational and employment opportunities.

THE MANPOWER ROUTE

There is a whole system of occupational training and work experience and vocational rehabilitation and education programs. Many new efforts have been launched to aid education from pre-school to graduate school. At long last we have discovered our giant cities, destined to grow bigger and to house three-quarters of us in another ten years. We have recognized that they are over-sized and underplanned, but unless our basic human capital is educated, healthy, and happy, we will have contributed to, not alleviated, these sores on the skin of our country.

The key human resource element in the total cluster may be direct occupational training for work at a subprofessional level—what we refer to as manpower training.

The Manpower and Development Training Act of 1962 is only one of more than 30 acts which provide in some part for training. Congress thought of it as a broad and flexible foundation stone of a national manpower policy. Its yearly polishing by Congress has been done almost with loving care.

The Manpower Act was first addressed in 1962 to a condition of high unemployment—approximately 7 percent—in which automation was seen as a heavy cause. The word "automation" was used somewhat loosely then, covering all of the reasons why a man's usefulness was cut when a developing technology constantly escalated the levels of skill demands.

The fear of automation creating a strong force for unemployment fortunately has not materialized yet. But there is still an uncomfortable percentage locked in and locked out of our society for lack of any skill to do a job. Beyond this, jobs are changing at a rapid pace. Peter Drucker, one of America's foremost management specialists, has pointed out that "Since we live in an age of innovation, a practical education must prepare a man for work that does not yet exist and cannot yet be clearly defined." The U.S. Department of Labor reports increased needs for skilled workers and observes that employees in many if not most job categories can expect to retrain, perhaps several times during their working careers, as occupational requirements change.

Grant Venn, Associate Commissioner of Education for Adult and Vocational Education, has pointed out that

> We are the first generation who must help educate young people to a new dimension of time and change. Solutions to problems of our society 50 years ago have almost no bearing on solutions to current problems. In six years, the labor force has moved from a majority in production to a majority in distribution and services occupations. Man will need to change jobs four or five times during his life's work, so that preparation for specific job skills is simply not defensible.

Dr. Harold Stevens, a neurologist, in a commencement address to graduating medical students, said: "You have prepared here—but for what? There is only one answer: preparation for change. Aim at a moving target—hope you'll be prepared to change your course. Much learning will be forgotten or archaic in a few years, degraded into useless half-truths or worse." Henrik Ibsen said: "The value of a truth lasts about 15 years and then it rots into error." The present store of medical knowledge has a half-life of about five years. Alfred N. Whitehead put it succinctly: "Information, like fish, does not keep too long."

Training and retraining, therefore, will be a permanent part of everyone's life in a full-employment economy and must accompany the fiscal and monetary measures also necessary to create jobs. The full-employment economies in Western Europe have discovered this and plan for one percent of the work force to be in training at all times. More and more individuals must get periodic training through a working life.

TRAIN AND EAT

But how can people and their dependents live during the time it takes to get training, especially if it should stretch out into months? It seems clear that heads of households need at least a minimal allowance.

The Manpower Act recognizes that whenever education or training is necessary to make an individual self-supporting, it is a social cost, not a private, personal one. This is actually a social investment rather than a cost, because it pays for itself with generous interest. Selma Mushkin, economist, proposes a sabbatical for every worker at age 35 to allow him to refurbish his skills or learn new work, to be paid for out of Social Security benefits. Other new devices for underwriting necessary training costs may include their consideration as a fringe benefit in labor contracts, insurance systems, or other means in addition to direct governmental support.

READING, WRITING, AND TRAINING

At one time individuals could learn jobs, even those requiring considerable manual dexterity and skill, without having much competence in basic literacy and arithmetic. This is becoming increasingly more difficult. Even a custodian has to be able to read labels, instructions, manuals, and other printed material, and at least a fair arithmetic competence may be essential. Amendments to the Act now extend training time to permit basic literacy or other prevocational training to whatever extent necessary to make occupational training possible. In the long run, it is to be hoped that other supports now given to general elementary and secondary education and the development of new methodologies in education will bring people to adult life without the necessity for so much remediation. Despite a substantial rise in educational attainment, one-third of the adults will lack high school diplomas in 1985, and even as close as 1975, millions in the labor force will have no more than an eighth grade education; and we have learned that there is a distressing shrinkage from grade level completed to performance level. Today we find that one out of three people with only eighth grade education is unemployed; one of six with high school education is unemployed, while only one of twenty-two with a college degree is unemployed. It is estimated that 7.5 million of the 26 million youngsters looking for jobs in the next decade will be school dropouts. The principle is therefore now established: We have a social responsibility to give everybody the basic competencies he needs.

ANYONE CAN LEARN

The question in the past has been, Is this possible for *everyone?* It has often been assumed that laziness, lack of will, or lack of intrinsic ability and aptitude preclude a sizable number of people from ever getting anywhere. We are learning through manpower programs that this is largely a myth. Traditional education is not the whole answer, and its efficiency can be drastically improved. Sociologists and psychologists have demonstrated in depressed areas, both rural and urban, that a certain ecology can breed disability and visit the sins of ignorance, toil, and poverty on the children of generations. Nevertheless, in some of those environments it has been possible to take total illiterates—adults buffeted by defeat and despair—and find enough resilience and substance to bring them from zero to fifth grade competence in three months. Some of the experimental and demonstration projects under the Manpower Act have proved that in education we know only what we have done—we do not yet know what we can do. A malfunctioning individual must therefore be viewed as a challenge, not a discard.

Manpower training has pioneered the concept of giving the training at any time of the year in a direct, practical, high-intensity form to get the man on a payroll as soon as possible. A family man out of work, in need of training or retraining, cannot wait three months until the next semester of school opens, and then—even with some subsistence allowance—take another year or so to learn a job.

The range of occupations for which public education has now assumed a responsibility is open-ended. The Manpower Act has pioneered this, and other measures will continue to support it. Without an expansion of choices and a freedom of choice, we would plunge immediately into a radical centralism of technocratic control. It would be the end of democracy and back to exploitation.

In this connection, support for labor mobility has become essential. The 1965 amendments to the Manpower Act started, and the 1966 ones continue, provision for experimental support to people to change locale of living to accept new job opportunities. The principle has been accepted. It remains to develop the feasibilities and practical means.

HEALTHY AND WISE

Mark Twain once wrote: "Training is everything. The peach was once a bitter almond; cauliflower is nothing but cabbage with a college education." But poor health and chronic physical ail-

ments are some of the chief causes of inability to take or continue
in training. The 1966 amendments to the Manpower Act provide
for more effort to get health remediation from existing sources and
to supplement them further, up to a cost of $100 per trainee if
necessary. Again other measures may have to come along to support the principle enshrined here, but the principle is now recognized: A person must not languish in a correctable physical disability that prevents him from education or training and hence
economic self-support. Thus manpower development and training is an evolving program, shaped by Congress and the Administration to meet evolving or changing needs.

THE HUMAN DIMENSION

Ralph McGill, noted columnist, described the effects of automation in one industry:

> Six years ago, 10 per cent of South Carolina's cotton was machine-
> picked. When cotton picking time comes around within a few weeks,
> 90 per cent will be machine-picked. Men, women and children who
> were needed six years ago are surplus humanity. . . . The workers,
> many of them grandchildren . . . are cast off—penniless, illiterate,
> homeless. . . .
>
> The unemployed are condemned for being on welfare. The myth
> persists that they would "rather" be on welfare than work. That is not
> true. What is true is that a jobless, unskilled, illiterate person on
> welfare . . . won't quit it to pick cotton for $3 a day for a few weeks—
> and then be off welfare *and* out of work. . . .
>
> The situation is one of human beings, long neglected and eco-
> nomically helpless. It requires the best of us.

This is the challenge to all of those engaged in training manpower. Our programs have been marked with a high degree of
general success. For this, many are to be congratulated. But there
is more to be done. Our work begins, not ends, with this success.

We must go beyond the goal of just training a person who
seeks our services or merely getting him placed on a job. As the
HEW 1966 report, "Education and Training," states: "The *acid*
test for success in the manpower training program—or any other
training program—is employment after training and the capability
of retaining a job. . . . Since the start of the program 77 percent
of the graduates have obtained training-related jobs." The record
in these terms seems good.

Setting aside the question of the other 23 percent and why
they did not get employment in training-related jobs, or employment at all, the question is: Have we finished our work when that

77 percent get employed? Should we be content that we have helped a large number of citizens and let it go at that?

Upward Mobility

Our task is not over when we have found someone a *job* after training; we should then be concentrating our efforts on helping the individual to a *career*. We seem to assist the middle-class and prosperous child or adult in terms of long-range series of occupational and educational experiences which permit relevant choices to be made at critical periods and better chances for upward socioeconomic mobility; while for the very poor, those disadvantaged Americans we see in many of the manpower programs, we tend to look at very short-range goals, a job, and to stop there.

Usually the job is an entry level position in a plant or business. What are the subsequent opportunities for the person we place? Is he motivated toward advancement? Are his aspirations less significant than those of the high school or college graduate? Who is looking out for his interests, once we and the employer tick off another placement statistic?

We have much work to do, both with the person we place and with his employer. What additional training does he need to help him adjust to the job, demonstrate appropriate work attitudes, and be productive? What conditions for upgrading exist in the company? Are there restrictive policies which preclude promotion even when it is deserved? Do we attempt to work with employers and unions to facilitate upward mobility for our graduates? Sometimes we do, but not often enough. For we have served our clients poorly if we place them in the lowest jobs and forget them; we have stripped them of some measure of dignity if we say that they have a right to a job but not to a good job; we have deceived them if we treat them as short-range problems and not as long-range career challenges. And in the process we have cheated our country by depriving it of the utilization of every individual's highest level of skill.

One's work is one of the most important functions of his life, yet its meaning tends to be submerged in the production of one tally on a statistician's chart or one punch on a computer technician's card. If we must produce statistics, let us go beyond today's chart of placements made or even length of time on the job after placement, and let us present where these people go as a group in terms of advancement, earnings, or the other indications of success that we as middle-class Americans attach to our efforts. When we see progress here, we may feel truly satisfied that we have been really successful in accomplishing the substance of our jobs.

We may look at our efforts now not just in terms of solving problems of unemployment or of the inner city or of the Negro, all of which are to the good, but in the frame of reference of creating the conditions in which one human being can achieve satisfaction in being productive, being *allowed* to stretch his own abilities and to share in the birthright of every American—to see rewards and recognition for his own best efforts.

THE CHALLENGE

We have a reasonably clear goal and some generally defined guidelines. Manpower conditions are at last being seen by the planning specialists as changing, volatile, and diffuse. No longer will we let ourselves simply respond after the fact to manpower shortages and surpluses in our economy. The future must be anticipated and programs for attacking them must in effect be stockpiled and ready to be applied *before* the stark reality of unemployment faces our citizens. Longer-range manpower forecasting, guidance and counseling, and a modern, relevant program of vocational education are mandatory elements in keeping the supply and demand in viable relationship to each other. But we have much to learn in theory and technique. We must teach better and more efficiently. We must coordinate programs in more productive ways, for neither our time nor our money is unlimited. We must become ever more ingenious in planning and developing the capabilities of our federal and state law systems.

We must use freedom and imagination. This is a most crucial time in history. In fact, we dare not fail. All that we as a nation have strived together to build in our new federal and state and local partnership can soon come to naught if we do not provide the personnel that these new programs urgently require. The war on poverty and the recent new commitments in health and in education require an abundance of trained and motivated workers. The time is now to lay broad, firm, unshakable foundations for human resource development.

✳

Racial Barriers in Apprentice Training Programs

✳

IRVING KOVARSKY

TWO SIGNIFICANT EVENTS HAVE PAVED THE WAY FOR A NUMBER OF sequential economic changes and a "new" look at minority problems. The 1930 depression led to extensive criticism of micro-economic solutions to business problems and the laissez-faire governmental approach to private industry. Instead, the Keynesian solution to economic problems was favored, an approach necessitating government manipulation of industry and unions. Then World War II spotlighted the distinct economic disadvantage of the Negro. These two events, at least to some extent, led to overall prosperity; accelerated the importance of industry and technology while deflating the importance of agriculture and the rural area; increased labor mobility, occupational and geographic, for the Negro and white person; led to open Negro dissatisfaction with prejudice; and triggered an assault on discrimination by the executive and judicial branches of federal government, leading to fair employment laws.

The Negro, beginning with World War I, left the South for the North in increasing numbers. Whereas the bulk of our Negro

---

IRVING KOVARSKY is Professor of Industrial Relations and Law at the University of Iowa, Iowa City, Iowa.

population was concentrated in the agricultural South prior to World War I, approximately 73 percent are northern and southern urban dwellers at the present time.[1] But 54 percent of all Negroes still live in the South.[2] For those interested in training the Negro, it must be remembered that the transition from a field hand to a skilled worker in industry is painful, particularly when early education has been neglected. Training policy must take this into account. And many Negroes are first-generation urban dwellers.

The Negro made political headway in the South after the Civil War, and economic opportunity could have followed. Unfortunately the political gain was short lived. Negro deprivation, political and economic, was nearly complete by 1900. This development was anticipated by de Tocqueville, who observed prior to the Civil War:

> The Indians will perish in the same isolated conditions in which they have lived, but the destiny of the Negroes is in some measure interwoven with that of the European. These two races are fastened to each other without intermingling; and they are unable to separate entirely or to combine.
>
> . . . .
>
> Whoever has inhabited the United States must have perceived that in those parts of the Union in which the Negroes are no longer slaves they have in no wise drawn nearer to the whites. On the contrary, the prejudice of race appears to be stronger in the states that have abolished slavery than in those where it still exists; and nowhere is it so intolerant as in those states where servitude has never been known.
>
> . . . .
>
> If I were called upon to predict the future, I should say that the abolition of slavery in the South will . . . increase the repugnance of the white population for the black.[3]

De Tocqueville's observations are pertinent today. The Revolutionary War was presumably fought to attain liberty and colonial control over economic and political affairs. Certainly Washington and Jefferson recognized man's need for some voice and participation in his society. While openly acknowledging the evils of slavery, neither Washington nor Jefferson was willing to free his slaves after the Revolutionary War. Apparently morality is for-

---

[1] *Hearings on H.R. 405 and Similar Bills Before the Subcommittee on Labor of the House Committee on Education and Labor*, 88th Cong., 1st Sess. (1963).

[2] U.S. Dept. of Labor, *The Negroes in the United States, Their Economic and Social Situation*, Bul. 1511, 1966, p. 1.

[3] Alexis de Tocqueville, *Democracy in America*, Vol. I, New York: Mentor Paperback, 1960, pp. 370, 373, 390.

98 *Irving Kovarsky*

gotten to protect assets. To end slavery, strong government leadership was essential and a war had to be fought. Although the Civil War ended slavery, intolerance remained the rule rather than the exception, and government intervention was later necessary to end "badges of servitude." It must be fully understood that the North was unwilling to tolerate slavery, but there was never any intention of accepting the Negro as an equal.

To establish more recent injury to the Negro: In 1950, 4.6 percent of our white population were unemployed while 8.5 percent of our nonwhite population faced unemployment. In 1953, 3.6 percent of the white population and 7.9 percent of our Negro citizens were without work. By 1960, 5 percent of the white work force compared to 10.2 percent of the Negro laboring element were unemployed. In 1962, it was 4.9 percent compared to 11 percent; in 1963, 5.1 percent compared to 10.9 percent; in 1964, 4.6 percent compared to 9.8 percent; and 4.6 percent compared to 9.2 percent in 1965.[4] These figures are enlightening in view of the legislative, executive, and judicial protection accorded the Negro since World War II. In spite of the protective blanket, difficulty was experienced moving the Negro into skilled jobs.

Based on 1960 Census data in Iowa, 3.1 percent of the white and 9.3 percent of the nonwhite population were unemployed.[5] Since few Negroes in Iowa are farming, the problem is urban and industrial. It is interesting to note that in 1960 the Negro unemployment rate throughout the United States was twice that of the white population while in Iowa the ratio was three to one.

SOME BASIC ASSUMPTIONS

To provide a meaningful framework for discussion, it is fitting at this point to indulge in several assumptions which seem realistic as well as pertinent.

First, job openings requiring skill will be made available to the Negro *slowly* and *grudgingly*. Opportunities for the development of skill will come *slowly* because:
1. Many Negroes lack a basic education so that training is more difficult.
2. Negroes fail to take advantage of available opportunity because of a basic distrust of the white-dominated firm. Many Negroes feel that the white person will continue to discriminate in spite of statements and policy to the contrary.
3. Because of failures in public school and elsewhere, some Ne-

[4] Herald Tribune, *The U.S. Book of Facts, Statistics, and Information*, 1966, Table 300, p. 218.
[5] U.S. Bureau of Census, *United States Census of Population, 1960*, Table 53.

groes lack confidence in their ability to successfully complete a training program.
4. Negroes living in a segregated world are unaware of existing opportunities.

Openings for the Negro will come *grudgingly* because:

1. Racial discrimination in employment has been a way of life in the United States almost from its inception and startling changes in the attitudes of white people cannot be anticipated. With the legal and mounting social onslaught on discrimination, prejudice is driven underground and not, as some feel, abated.
2. In some unions and industries, discrimination is more prevalent than in others.

If this observation is correct, federal and state authorities will have to constantly and forcefully pursue white employers and unions to assure employment equality.

The second assumption is that Negro unrest and dissatisfaction will continue and possibly increase in spite of signs of some progress. Negro dissatisfaction will continue because:

1. With little overall improvement in his economic lot since the end of slavery, making amends will prove difficult even under the best of conditions—there is too much "water under the bridge" to anticipate the rapid rectification of a grossly unjust situation.
2. Negro attitudes must be examined in light of the economic structure that exists today. Approximately 50 years ago, the skilled worker held a unique position within his community, an elite among the working class. Immigrants coming to the United States who managed to reach the status of a skilled worker experienced self-satisfaction and local respect. Although interested in moving into the professional or entrepreneurial sects, a failure to spring upward was not on a par with a lack of success. The Negro today is neither an immigrant nor a newcomer to industry.

It is a paradox that the Negro, for the first time in the history of the United States, can look forward to holding jobs requiring skill; yet, contrary to the white immigrant, he will not experience a corresponding satisfaction. Over the years, the prestige of the skilled worker has waned, and reaching the nirvana of industry today means entrance into the professional and managerial ranks.

Union Discrimination

Traditionally, unions affiliated with the AFL have displayed a greater taste for discrimination than have industrial type unions.

Although Gompers and Strasser professed moderate racial views, the AFL unfortunately was founded at a time when employer and government hostility toward unions prevented a climate more favorable to the Negro; survival was of foremost concern initially. After racial discrimination is tolerated within an organization, halting and changing the climate is difficult, frequently more difficult than its elimination at the inception.[6] Many of the AFL unions either excluded Negroes or operated segregated locals; but irrespective of the tactical design, Negroes were kept from skilled jobs. Until 1964, the NLRB could not find a sign of unfair representation merely because unions were lily-white or segregated. Although condemning racial discrimination in recent years, federation leaders have not been able to change substantially traditional practices although slight improvement is evident.

The discriminatory pattern of the CIO differed from that of the AFL. The basic industries were organized by the CIO during the 1930 depression, and Negroes holding the less desirable and unskilled jobs in the steel, rubber, and automobile industries were wooed to assure the right of representation. After industrial unions gained a toehold, the Negro was not encouraged, and in fact was sometimes discouraged, from seeking skilled jobs. However, strong feeling persists that employers rather than industrial unions were responsible for the bulk of the discrimination. In any event, neither the AFL nor the CIO permitted Negro participation at the skilled job level.

Not too long ago, more than one-half of the Negroes qualifying as skilled workers were attached to the building trades.[7] In fact, the Negro in the South dominated the building trades but gradually was squeezed out of jobs requiring skill and banished to the general labor category. In northern communities the Negro was always excluded from holding skilled jobs in construction. The plumbers, carpenters, electricians, steamfitters, and other trade unions have always "sat" on the Negro, and ending this exclusionary pattern is difficult. Some of these unions today have admitted Negroes.

Faced with a labor shortage during World War I, railroad operators convinced the southern Negro that an industrial nirvana awaited him in the North. By 1924, 136,065 Negroes found employment on the lines as common laborers.[8] In addition, 6,478 Negroes

[6] Hughes Tool Co., 56 L.R.R.M. 1289 (1964).
[7] Herbert R. Northrup, *Organized Labor and the Negro,* New York: Harper & Bros., 1944, pp. 5–8.
[8] "Employment of Negroes on Railroads," *Monthly Labor Rev.* 19:1105, 1924.

were employed as firemen. Due to technological changes and a dying industry, the Negro was soon restricted to the less desirable railroad jobs and was rendered nonpromotable by union and employer agreement. In some instances the Negro was pushed out of jobs which he traditionally held.

By 1930, more than 22 national unions barred Negroes from membership by constitutional stipulation; by 1943, the number was reduced to 13.[9] In 1960, only three national unions, railroad brotherhoods, formally barred the Negro from membership. Today the constitutional exclusion of Negroes from unions is unknown; this is due to laws outlawing discrimination and not to basic changes in attitude in many instances.

To establish the extent and difficulty of ending racial discrimination in the construction trade unions, a look at the problem in New York is enlightening. Although the New York law forbidding discrimination in employment was enacted in 1945, only in the past few years, and after considerable pressure, was a token number of Negroes admitted into the construction trade unions.

Unions with a taste for discrimination erect the following barriers to the admittance of Negro apprentices:

1. New members, as a condition of admittance, may be required to be related to old members. Where the past membership is all or mostly white, Negroes cannot enter unions and training programs.[10]

   The notion of relationship as a condition of membership is related to the hereditary fiefdom. In some European countries, children will follow the trade practiced by a father, a practice occurring infrequently in the United States.

2. In 1961, the Supreme Court decided that a hiring hall contract was legal under the Taft-Hartley Act, providing that union and nonunion people were referred to employers by unions.[11] The Supreme Court, to back its opinion, reasoned that unions were sometimes the only available source of skilled labor. Accepting the employer's need for the hiring hall, it is sometimes in use where discrimination is evident and the Negro is hurt by such an arrangement.

3. A few unions demand employer sponsorship before permitting

[9] Paul H. Norgren and Samuel E. Hill, *Toward Fair Employment*, New York: Columbia University Press, 1964, p. 41.

[10] Lefkowitz v. Farrell, 3 CCH State Lab. L. Rep., Par. 49996.81, (N.Y. SLRB, 1964).

[11] Local 357, Int. Bro. of Teamsters v. NLRB, 365 U.S. 667 (1961). In this case, the Supreme Court approved of the legality of the hiring hall.

apprentice training.[12] If this arrangement is used to discriminate, the union shifts responsibility to employer.
4. Apprentice training programs may be regulated in a manner
detrimental to the Negro interest.[13] For example, tests to determine eligibility can be used in a discriminatory fashion.[14]

The union viewpoint is interesting. Many members fear an
oversupply of skilled labor so that few apprentices are registered.
Although society may be interested in an adequate supply of labor in the future, members are only concerned with their current
well-being. For example, in the construction industry in 1964, the
unemployment rate was 9.9 percent compared to the overall rate
of 4.7 percent.[15] Conceding the position taken by members holding to a restrictive admittance policy, this does not excuse discrimination, and the closed shop is an illegal form of union security.

Unions also claim that few Negroes have the basic education
and qualifications necessary to enter the skilled trades and Negroes
quit before completing the apprenticeship period.

EMPLOYER DISCRIMINATION

The Negro in the North has been able to find employment—
the less desirable jobs—in the railroad, meat packing, shipbuilding,
iron and steel, and other industries. The Negro during World War
II made the most significant advance in acquiring skills in the
shipyards.[16] The demand for ships during a global war is almost
insatiable, and Negroes were welcomed into the shipyards. In addition, executive orders banning discrimination added to the protective cloak and advancement occurred.[17] Unfortunately most of
the jobs were of a temporary nature.

Being the least skillful and the last hired, the Negro was hard
hit by the 1930 depression. Overlooked by most critics is that the
industrial incentive to teach the Negro a skilled trade was missing
during the 1930 depression—there was already an overabundance
of skilled labor. Neither employers nor unions were interested in

[12] Int. Bro. of Electrical Workers, Local 35 v. Commission on Civil Rights,
Conn. Superior Court, 1954.
[13] Irving Kovarsky, "Apprentice Training Programs and Racial Discrimination," *Iowa Law Rev.* 50:755, 1965.
[14] Irving Kovarsky, "The Harlequinesque Motorola Decision and Its Implications," *Boston College Industrial and Commercial Law Rev.* 7:535, 1966.
[15] U.S. Conf. of Mayors, *Changing Employment Practices in the Construction Industry,* 1965, p. 6.
[16] Fair Employment Practice Committee, *First Report,* July 1943 to Dec.
1944, pp. 86–87.
[17] Irving Kovarsky, "Racial Discrimination in Employment and the Federal
Law," *Oregon Law Rev.* 38:54, 58, 1958.

training help already available. If the federal government had undertaken the training of Negroes, a responsibility easily assumed since the WPA program was initiated to provide work and place money into the hands of the "fast spender," a source of skilled labor would have been available during World War II and subsequently. Unfortunately a government only recently shifting from laissez-faire to Keynesian policy, and hampered by a depression and by a judicial attitude that the Constitution forbids government and not industry discrimination,[18] is not in a position to undertake programming helpful to the Negro.

During World War II, the Fair Employment Practices Committee, created by executive order,[19] considered charges of discrimination against some of the largest firms—Bethlehem Shipbuilding Company, Vultee Aircraft Company, Western Cartridge Company, A. O. Smith Corp., Nordberg Mfg. Co., Allis Chalmers Corp., Douglas Aircraft Corp., Lockheed Aircraft Corp., Carnegie-Illinois Steel Corp., Jones & Laughlin Steel Corp., Youngstown Sheet and Tube Co., etc. Experience during World War II illustrated the extent of employer discrimination and the need for government intervention if the Negro was to be accepted as an industrial equal.

OTHER FACTORS AFFECTING THE NEGRO

A factor which adds to current friction even though the cause is not racial is the increasing use of white female labor.[20] Since 1950, more than 50 percent of our total labor is supplied by the female, and an increase appears imminent. Because of war conditions and the expansion of white-collar employment, while the demand for unskilled labor drops or shifts, the male Negro competes with the opposite sex for jobs readily filled by the female. For example, the growth in jobs in New York City, a financial rather than industrial center, falls within the white-collar category, and the female Negro experiences less difficulty securing employment than the male Negro. Consequently the job explosion has not, proportionately, benefited the male Negro in New York. Due to the 1964 Civil Rights Act which forbids discrimination on the basis of sex[21] and the increasing dissatisfaction of the female who is

[18] Civil Rights Cases, 109 U.S. 3 (1883).
[19] *Ibid.*, pp. 58–60.
[20] Otis D. Duncan and Beverly Duncan, *The Negro Population of Chicago,* Chicago: University of Chicago Press, 1957; Herbert R. Northrup and Richard L. Rowan, *The Negro and Employment Opportunities,* Ann Arbor: University of Michigan Press, 1965, p. 364; Eli Ginzburg, *The Negro Potential,* New York: Columbia University Press, 1956, p. 27.
[21] Section 703 (a) and (d).

confined to the home and who is finding increased social approval for a business career, the percentage of females permanently attached to the work force should increase. Unless a determined and well-directed effort is made to ensure training for male Negroes where the female is not readily used, such as in trades where physical strength is necessary as well as skill, the future promises some difficulty. My emphasis on training male Negroes for jobs of a skilled and physical nature is based on the assumption that the female will desire to retain her femininity and not seek to develop muscle.

There is currently some indication that men are beginning to invade in greater number fields traditionally occupied by women —like social work, teaching, library science, etc. If this occurs, women may be seeking employment in the less traditional fields, which could be detrimental to the Negro in the short run.[22]

Another negative factor is the feasibility of training the Negro who is, let us say, 45 years or over. Based upon the number of years required in training and the fact that many of them come with a poor educational background, there is some question as to what kind, if any, training should be initiated. Rather than train the elderly Negro, it may be wise to consider another approach such as a direct subsidy.

Many Negroes without the support of a stable family life find it difficult to hold on while in apprentice training. This becomes more acute where the apprenticeship is in an industry which is noted for seasonality and where years of training are required.

Further difficulty is promised because the number of nonwhite workers in the labor force will increase at a faster pace than white workers for the next 15 years.[23] The nonwhite work force will rise from 8.7 million to 12.3 million while white workers will increase from 69.7 to 89.1 million. Considering the current extent of Negro unrest together with providing additional opportunity for more people adds to the difficulty of finding adequate training solutions.

Another stumbling block is the firm and the type of training. Large firms frequently emphasize professional and technical training and encourage additional college course work during the evening.[24] On the other hand, smaller firms appear to be more interested in the training of skilled craftsmen. From a supervisory

[22] 63 L.R.R. 81 (9–26–66).

[23] 63 L.R.R. 103 (10–3–66).

[24] U.S. Dept. of Labor, "Training of Workers in American Industry," Report of a Nationwide Survey of Training Programs in Industry in 1962 by the Manpower Administration, Bureau of Apprenticeship and Training, 1964, pp. 10–11.

aspect, these data hit a vital nerve—keeping a watchful eye over a large number of small firms to assure Negro training is more difficult than keeping a "fatherly" eye on fewer firms substantial in size. As a means of combatting this difficulty, the Equal Employment Opportunity Commission (EEOC) can, per section 750 (g) (5) of the Civil Rights Act, conduct broad-scale investigations without the receipt of a complaint, acquiring data which can be publicized. Together with the Department of Labor, the EEOC could provide the necessary data essential to the enlightened manipulation of a training program. It is essential to recognize that relying on individual FEP complaints does not provide mass openings.

In the construction trades, unions often control the apprentice training programs. But in finance, insurance, and real estate, industries in which discrimination abounds, employers generally assume the responsibility of training employees. It is estimated that 34 percent of the firms in finance, insurance, and real estate sponsor some type of training program.[25] Public officials, aware of the focal point of discrimination, must periodically review, without the receipt of a complaint, the records of the union or employer. In further consolidating the data reviewed, promoting the hiring of the male Negro where the female worker is strongly entrenched is not advisable unless a large job expansion is contemplated.

In fairness to the finance, insurance, and real estate industries, the doors are slowly being opened to Negro employment.

Another burden is the federal law. After bitter debate and years of consideration, Congress enacted the Civil Rights Act in which several provisions outlaw discrimination in apprentice training. Section 703 (a) forbids an employer "to fail or refuse to hire . . . or otherwise discriminate against any individual," while section 703 (b) outlaws the limitation, segregation, or classification of employees in a discriminatory manner. Although sections 703 (a) and (b) do not refer to apprentice training, the language is broad enough to reach discrimination at this level. In addition, section 703 (d) specifically prohibits employer and union discrimination while operating an apprentice training program. Section 703 (j) protects the employer unwilling "to grant preferential treatment to any individual or to any group . . . on account of an imbalance which may exist." Many feel that the Negro is entitled to "preferential treatment." *Unless concessions are made and immediate needs appreciated, the Negro will not penetrate the skilled job levels in sufficient number*. Negroes find section 703 (j) unpalatable and tokenism

---

[25] *Ibid.*, p. 18.

intolerable. In light of the shortage of skilled labor and Negro unrest, section 703 (j) should be repealed. Currently the will of Congress conflicts with the needs of the Negro.

Section 703 (j) is not apropos or restrictive where the employer,
without coercion, is willing "to grant preferential treatment" to
the Negro. However, the white person injured by the preference
could possibly claim reverse discrimination, which is prohibited by
federal law.

The Iowa FEPC law, section 7, provides:

(1) It shall be an unfair or discriminatory practice for any:

a. Person to refuse to hire, accept, register, classify, or refer for employment, to discharge any employee, or to otherwise discriminate in
employment against any applicant for employment or any employee
because of the race, creed, color, national origin, or religion of such
applicant or employee.

b. Labor organization or the employee, agents, or members therefore
to refuse to admit to membership any applicant, to expel any member,
or to otherwise discriminate against any applicant for membership
or any member, in the privileges, rights, or benefits of such membership because of the race, creed, color, national origin, or religion of
such applicant or member.[26]

The Iowa law is broad enough to outlaw discrimination in apprentice training programs.

Some Current Data

The Bureau of Labor statistics estimate that white-collar jobs
will grow twice as fast as blue-collar jobs during the next ten years;
it is anticipated that white-collar employment will rise 38 percent
while blue-collar employment will rise by 17 percent. At the same
time, employment in services should rise by 35 percent and jobs on
farms should decline by 21 percent. There is anticipated a 54 percent rise in the need for professional workers.[27] These data are
encouraging in terms of helping the Negro—the lone exception is
the 21 percent decline in agricultural jobs. Negroes will be hard
hit because of added competition from the white farm workers who
will move to industry and more Negroes will be forced to shift to
urban areas.

It was also reported that "Within the blue-collar categories,

[26] 25 S.L.L. 117.
[27] 63 L.R.R. 81 (9–26–66).

employment gains by 1975 are expected for all major occupations with the exception of bakers, compositers, typesetters, and machine-tool operators. Among skilled workers, job gains will be particularly large for business-machine servicemen, cement and concrete finishers, road-machinery operators, plumbers, pipefitters, and television and appliance servicemen."[28]

The same report estimates that "contract construction will rise by 37 percent . . . while the gain in manufacturing will come to 14 percent. Within manufacturing, the sharpest increases in jobs will be 38 percent in instruments, 34 percent in rubber, 29 percent in electrical equipment, 28 percent in nonelectrical machinery and chemicals, 26 percent in furniture, and 24 percent in paper."

As of March, 1966, nonwhite workers remained at 11 percent of the total work force, 21 percent of the unemployed, and 25 percent of the long-term unemployed.[29] Between 1962 and 1965, Negroes seemed to make the most significant gains in the professional, craft, and sales categories. However, they made the least significant gains in the managerial ranks.[30]

The Negro is seldom found in positions of command. He will probably find it much easier to crack the ranks of the professional in large numbers than the managerial class. Many white people will accept the Negro as an employee of equal rank but not as an overseer and leader, an attitude which will be more difficult to break in the South than in the North.

SUMMARY

The Negro today is an urban dweller whose well-being is tied to industry. The latest available data show that in such heavily populated cities as New York, Chicago, Philadelphia, Baltimore, Newark, and Los Angeles, the Negro has not gained percentagewise in the existing economic bounty as in other places.

Putting together the available data where discrimination seems to continue and assuming the anticipated demand for labor, the federal government should concentrate its training efforts on the big city. For example, if the demand for construction will continue at a high level as anticipated, government concentration on the urban centers can maximize the possibility of Negro entrance into

[28] *Ibid.*
[29] U.S. Dept. of Labor, *The Negroes In the U.S., Their Economic and Social Situation,* Bul. 1511, 1966, p. 9.
[30] *Ibid.,* pp. 26–29.

the skilled trades because the bulk of the construction work is let to urban firms.

In the society in which we live, we can anticipate a growing imbalance between jobs skills required in the future and those needed at the present time. Future jobs will require more skill, and Negro training must be geared to future needs rather than present needs.

✹

Physical and Mental Barriers

✹

JAMES W. HARRINGTON

MANPOWER DEVELOPMENT IS A TERM WHICH HAS RECEIVED SOME prominence in recent years. It is a term, however, that has never had too much appeal for me. As we listen to proposals that we should train the unskilled to become skilled, and train the skilled to become highly skilled, and so forth, we should realize that, rightly or wrongly, these discussions concern a concept that has an objective of designing or redesigning people to fit the requirements of our economic and social systems. Our economic and social systems have, of course, enabled us to produce more material comforts for more people than any other system in existence, and certainly I do not want to debunk training, education, or counseling. But we do have our shortcomings, and I believe we must never forget that our systems exist to protect and support the people and not vice versa. Mr. Socknat (Chapter 1) makes a fine distinction between a manpower policy and a human resources policy: "The crux of the difference is in the limitation of the manpower policy to labor market activity whereas an active human resources policy would recognize the intrinsic value of human resources and would

JAMES HARRINGTON is a member of the Board of Control of State Institutions, State of Iowa, Des Moines, Iowa.

systematize the programs of human resources, conservation, development, and utilization for ends beyond ensuring an orderly demand-supply equilibrium of full employment."

This kind of policy appeals to me. Mr. Socknat has said he does not know how to achieve this specifically, and neither do I, but the concept of a human resources development policy as distinct from manpower development policies is very interesting. I would hope, as suggested by Professor Boulding (Chapter 4), that we will rechannel some of our brain power into this area of need and develop methods of implementing a national policy of human resources development. I would hope, too, that our concept of productivity can be redefined and extended to include more than material production.

Let me give you a small illustration. Some years ago I visited rather frankly with a successful businessman. He was perhaps not a typical businessman, but he had an ulcer and a tight look on his face which perhaps was brought on by his rather total reluctance to let go of *anything*. He wasn't really a very happy person, but there was one bright spot in his life—a ten-year-old niece who was mentally retarded. This little girl's simple, straightforward, and open demonstration of love and affection for him meant more to him, he said, than just about anything else. Now who was more productive in this relationship? And yet because our society places its values where it does on material and technological accomplishments, this girl would be seen by most persons as a liability. Who needs developing most—she or we?

My assignment is to discuss and answer questions about physical and mental barriers to human resources development. Real progress has in fact been made in the care of the mentally ill in Iowa and in other states in the past ten years, and some of this progress is the result of technological and technical developments. But the really big changes that have taken place are not with the mentally ill at all but with us, with society, and in our social system. The first thing we did as a society was to discontinue putting sick people in an environment that could only make them sicker and holding them there for ten years. We discovered that it was not very helpful to put a lonely, depressed person who felt like ending it all in a bare, isolated cell. It might be better if he had someone to talk to, to take an interest in him and to encourage him through some of his rough periods. Most of the changes and progress have come about because society has been educated, counseled, and trained. We have overcome some of our fears and ignorance and prejudice in this regard, and this is where most of the progress in mental health has been made.

A number of years ago a group of us in Blackhawk County conducted a census of all the children from the county who were under the care of various agencies throughout the state. Among the items of identifying information was the question of race. In the assessment of these questionnaires, those agencies which were classified as correctional or mental health or child welfare all reported that 15–25 percent of their cases from our county were Negroes, but the Woodward State Hospital for the retarded stood out like a sore thumb in this. They reported only 3 percent of their cases were Negroes. Our first conclusion on this discrepancy was that Woodward must be discriminating against Negroes and discouraging their admission. Then there were other speculations, such as that this was some kind of a subcultural thing and that Negroes kept their retarded children at home, or that Negroes must be smarter than whites, or, conversely, that perhaps Negroes did not even recognize a retarded child when they saw one. Finally there was a realization of the obvious—that the 3 percent figure from Woodward was the only one that was consistent with the 4 percent rate of Negroes to whites in Blackhawk County at that time. It was the other figures that were disproportionately high. It is interesting that the consistency was in the problem area of mental deficiency, which is most likely to have a biological base, and the other problem areas where there was such a high rate of Negroes involved are most related to adverse environmental influences. There followed a long discussion of what should be done to improve the conditions for Negro children: more education, better education, counseling, perhaps some foster homes—almost everything that was remedial or correctional for Negro children but accepting them.

Training, education, retraining, and counseling are very good; but when our society refers to any so-called disadvantaged group— be it ADC recipients, mentally retarded, Negroes, the aged—and begins to prescribe training, education, counseling, and other remedies for their problems, we do so at the risk of rationalizing away our real social and moral problem, which is that we basically reject people who do not fit into our social norms, whatever they might be. We as a society are willing to do just about everything for those we label disadvantaged except the right thing, and that is to accept them for their own God-given worth and value.

✷

Institutional Barriers

✷

JAMES A. THOMAS

THE THREE DIFFERENT TOPICS I WILL DISCUSS AS INSTITUTIONAL BAR-
riers are law, custom, and what I call demographic patterns.

Law is the very thing that is intended to be the working force
in the midst of changes in cultural, economic, and societal patterns,
but law becomes institutionalized itself and becomes a barrier to
progress in the development of human resources. How is this accomplished? In one fashion the pronouncement of a law quite often
is mistaken to establish negatively those issues not specifically dealt
with by the language of the law. An example might be a law which
prohibits the stealing of lemons, oranges, and grapefruit. This can
be taken to mean that what this law really does is to encourage the
stealing of apples, because apples were not mentioned specifically, so
it is negatively implied that this is all right. This is a societal norm
that we will accept, because it is not covered in the law. So what
has actually developed is the use of the law for quite the contrary
purpose for which it was intended. This is what is happening to
Fair Employment Practices laws, public accommodations laws, and
housing laws. The argument seems to center more on whether or
not the specific question involved in a case is covered under the

---

JAMES THOMAS is Executive Director of the Iowa Civil Rights Commission,
Des Moines, Iowa.

law and on the technicality of whether we are dealing with something that is covered on the one hand or specifically endorsed on the other. The difficult problems are where the exceptions are to be placed. In fact the focal point in the law is on the exceptions rather than the import, the thrust of the law itself, what the law seems to do, the policy behind it.

Another problem is the general approach of the case-by-case method of operation. This is insufficient to deal with problems which have to be dealt with on a broader scale. For one thing there is a reluctance to complain by the people who are most directly affected by the factors with which the law was originally prescribed to deal. The individual really has no basis for comparing his situation and experience with those of other people. When he goes before an employer or a prospective employer, he has no way of knowing what the experience of others before him or subsequent to him has been or will be; he only knows what happened to him. Many of these people are the very people who were the subject matter of the law, but they simply do not know that they are victims. Also the case-by-case approach taxes the resources of the injured party, and very often, especially when we are dealing with laws that are designed to facilitate change, we are dealing with people with limited resources who do not have the capacity, the motivation to utilize the machinery of the law.

Another consideration is the very rigid and narrow construction or application of a law, so much so that the effect is to counteract the full impact and purpose of the law. An example of this is reverse discrimination. I have had some experience in working with the Civil Rights Division of the Department of Justice on voting registration matters, and a major question involved in the work there was how to bring about the necessary change in the societal structure and how to get large numbers of people, who heretofore had had no concern with civic responsibility, involved in the business of becoming responsible citizens. In order to do it, we had to take a law which said you may not discriminate in selecting candidates for voting and use that law to find a positive obligation on the part of the officials dealing with the law to go beyond nondiscrimination into the area of positive action to deal with problems that have occurred in the past.

My second category is custom. Traditional job categories which amount to customary examples of institutions limit our flexibility in discovering workable new solutions to old problems. Women's jobs, Negroes' jobs, college, high school, and dropout jobs are categories into which we very rigidly fit and pattern our existence so that they become barriers to the full utilization of all of our human resources. The customary training prerequisites also are barriers. Often the high school diploma is required in a situation that perhaps at the outset was reasonable but which, in the light of changing times, has become an out-of-date requirement for training. The college degree is demanded many times when we know the end result being sought is certainly out of keeping with this prerequisite for training. Another problem is that the work schedules to which we are accustomed are geared to a time when round-the-clock work was impossible. Consequently we have the work day, the work week, and the work year in many instances being unrealistic to our total labor pool. The school year is another interesting phenomenon.

Another problem of custom is the forced retirement of workers at an arbitrarily set age and the consequent destruction of our most highly seasoned and experienced human resources. We tell many of our productive workers that they must at a particular time in their development cease to be functional members of society and go off into retirement. The matters of prejudice, superstition, and what I call totalistic ignorance certainly frustrate the total development of human resources.

A final thing in terms of custom that is very important is the insufficient effort at all levels of our government. Today we are seeing the expansion of governmental effect throughout society. The government is the largest working company in the nation, and as such, it is the only company that is adequately equipped and adequately dispersed throughout the nation to deal with some of the very difficult problems of full utilization of our resources. Therefore, when the governmental structure makes an insufficient effort, it sometimes acts to frustrate the entire program and perhaps does more negatively than if we had done nothing. Here in Iowa we have a Civil Rights Act, the enactment of which was, in its inception, a step forward. I have been working with this act for some time and have been impressed with the fact that unless an organization can function meaningfully, there is severe question as to what total effect the law might have.

As for demographic patterns, I will suggest only a few of the topics within this very broad and difficult area. The central city in itself has become institutionalized to the degree that there are police problems, problems of mobility of the work force, problems of communication. We are erecting more and more barriers. The neighborhood concept is one that needs to be examined. Right along with the central city I will mention the suburbs. These two things, the city and the suburbs, suggest a multitude of problems.

Social and Spatial Barriers

RONALD C. POWERS

WE HAVE PRESENTED THE NOTION THAT HUMAN RESOURCE DEVELOP-
ment concepts have reflected heavily the notion of manpower development for the disadvantaged only, with an emphasis on the
"holy trinity" of employment, income, and political currency for
every politician. The thing I am concerned about is the concept of
environmental barriers to development suggested by Mr. Socknat
(Chapter 1). This concept includes such things as changes of resi-
dence, occupation, social setting, face-to-face associations, other institutions or roles and ways of acting, of experiences and expectations, and finally of personal memories, habits, and needs, including the need for more personal identity.

One social and spatial barrier that prevents us from achieving
personal needs has in fact already been identified: while we might
agree conceptually about the breadth and scope of what human resource development means, we tend in practice to be concerned primarily with those programs that lead to the trinity just mentioned.

A second barrier involves the meager efforts of public affairs
education. Until we as a society invest much more in the human

---

RONALD POWERS is an Associate Professor of Sociology at Iowa State University, Ames, Iowa.

capital sector which is aimed at understanding the social and economic system in which we operate, we will never seriously embrace such programs that will lead to making people really develop their human resources for living, for earnings, for consuming, and for being a part of this total society. Until our educational efforts are successful in getting all people, not just disadvantaged, to understand how our system operates, the instigation of specific programs aimed at various targets will continue to be difficult. There are many good solid citizens who are utterly ignorant about the causes and the implications regarding various programs and the possibilities of developing human resources, of what causes welfare problems, of the difference between human investment and maintenance cost, and the like.

Another barrier that we might put in the social and spatial category is the larger area utopia now being espoused whereby we come to a supermarket of social services that will be put in central cities to deal with all the problems under one roof. Many people are beginning to realize that political jurisdictions like town boundaries, incorporated limits, and county lines are outmoded; but it does not necessarily follow that all of the services for people, disadvantaged and otherwise, should also be located based on the criteria of economies of scale for a particular operation, for encompassing a larger number of clientele, and for an economic base that is large enough in which we can elicit local tax support in large part.

For example, if employment offices were concentrated in a central city and satellite offices eliminated under the illusion that we in the twentieth century travel further and faster than ever before, would the people who are the clients of this kind of service be the ones who are traveling further and faster? Another dimension is that we create evermore a solid image of bureaucracy for dealing with very human problems on the one hand, while certain other agencies and organizations are saying that we must begin to make the personal investment for personal relationships in solving very difficult problems.

The marginal cost concepts of economics and the ability of land to pay the cost seem to win out frequently when we decide where to place various institutions.

Another barrier is the planning and coordinating syndrome, which is a basic fear on the part of some people in our economy and society about the whole notion of planning and where it can lead us in terms of the values which we tend to hold central. Perhaps we have failed in the kind of training and background we put into developing planners to work with the concept of plan change. Too often (and this is an overgeneralization) we seem to invest a good deal of effort in training people to make sure we have the right number of restrooms per thousand tourists, the right amount of space for cars at the supermarket, the right kind of hedges to screen the junkyard; and not nearly enough attention is paid to the process by which people can be meaningfully involved in planning or in retaining this planning expertise throughout the process.

The occupation selection process (learning about occupations and how to decide which ones to go into) is another obstacle. We have only to look at the data for people who go to college, let alone those who do not, to know that we must have a pretty ineffective selection procedure. For instance, many students change curricula at least once or twice before finishing their first degree.

Another important part of human resource development is the work and income concept. Given the impact of greater leisure time, how are we to use it meaningfully? Other barriers are social class and social mobility. The more specific ones of values, attitudes, education, and environment are real barriers, but keep in mind that they are barriers to putting into operation almost any program we can design to help human beings and that some of the most resistent barriers are those that we ourselves have devised—the customs and laws that have brought about our values, attitudes, and demographic patterns.

✳

Questions From the Floor

QUESTION: You used the phrase: "values we hold central." What are the specific values that you feel must shift, change, or evolve to really implement human resource development?

RONALD POWERS: Recently we had occasion to ask a number of community leaders about their attitudes and opinions toward a number of things regarding social and economic development. One of the questions we asked was: "Which is more important, the war on poverty or economic development?" The unanimous answer was economic development. When we followed this up, there was no real sense of connection between trying to help people who categorized or qualified under the war on poverty and what would be economic development. When we followed it even further, a concern began to come out in terms of the number of people actually living on the land and what this means to the functioning of democratic society. Nobody has the answer as to whether we would cease to be a society if we went below some minimum level of people on the land. But when you follow this value, it gets to be the notion that wiggling your toes in the dirt is somehow better than the carpet, so that we have a high value here both on being attached to land as property and on being attached to the notion of work with an emphasis on the physical. Being attached then is another kind of value dimension which is a work-yourself-up-from-the-bottom value and anyone who is not on his way up the ladder has only himself to blame and not any happenstance of the system in which we live. We need to take a close look at those kinds of values. One thing we do not like to do is to classify our values and put them in a hierarchy. We would rather have them cafeteria style—all we want of everything. But the business of decision-making, whether it be in economic or social segments, demands that we somehow place a hierarchy on values.

QUESTION: Since there are so many subtleties inherent in the art of discrimination, should Civil Rights commissions wait for *provable* complaints before they take action? QUESTION: There are many trades in Iowa where there is a complete absence of Negroes. In addition, there is a great reluctance on the part of Negroes to apply for entrance in these trades. What is planned to overcome discrimination in this area where the possibility of complaint is very low?

JAMES THOMAS: I will begin by answering the first part of the question very simply. No. I do not think we should wait for provable complaints, because organizations such as the one I work for have the facilities to define a problem, first of all, which the individual does not have. We should take affirmative action and start to investigate a situation where there may not be, in the end result, a definition of a discriminator. We ought to focus on what the end result of the process might be. It is helpful (in the case of the trades) to get minority participation where heretofore there had been none, not simply to label the trade union involved as a discriminator. This is hard work. The problem is that the unions will partially admit that there have been difficulties in the past, but nobody really wants to make the effort to dig deep enough to locate the workers and get them to apply and take the training and go into the union halls. This has to be done by a concerted effort on the part of organizations like my own. Finally, the thrust of this question is very important because the process must not be viewed as one likened to a criminal process. This is what the opponents have often done to civil rights matters. They claim that we are trying to define criminals in our society. If that were the case, we could indict all of us. We could indict the United States of America and send us up for years, but we just want to try and get the people into jobs.

QUESTION: Faced with scarcity of resources, how practical is it to go beyond remedial manpower development programs into what has been referred to as human resource development?

JAMES HARRINGTON: Faced with the scarcity of manpower in resources, it is impractical to think only in terms of remedial programs. So that you will be aware of the kinds of costs that go into a
rehabilitative effort with a family that has disintegrated, I will use
an illustration. We talk about conservation of human resources.
In our public assistance programs, for instance, we insist that, before we help a family that is in difficulty, they not only *claim* that
they are failures and inadequate but they *prove* that they are inadequate—that they are failures in our social system. This is what
we call the means test. We want to be sure they are far enough
down before we extend any kind of a hand. And then we assess
through some vague standards what is the minimum amount of
help they need just to continue, and then we talk in terms of giving
them half or three-quarters of this amount. It takes a super strong
person to even survive on some of our assistance programs. If
they do not survive and the family really deteriorates—the father
throws in the towel and deserts, and the mother perhaps becomes
so upset through the process and the pressures on her that she winds
up in the state mental hospital, the father winds up in jail, and
the children wind up in institutions or foster care someplace. To
the extent that we try rehabilitative efforts in a situation like this,
we are talking about an investment in manpower to help families.
In institutional care, in an intensive program of rehabilitation for
an emotionally disturbed child, an outlay of $1,000 a month is not
at all uncommon. Just punishing a man by keeping him in a cell
at Anamosa costs $200 a month. And for the mother who is in some
mental hospital, we probably have an outlay of between $500 and
$700 a month. So for a given family we may be spending $5,000 or
$6,000 a month in a rehabilitation effort when it might have cost
$500 a month to help the family before it disintegrated. We ap-
parently just do not believe in conserving what is there; we just insist that when a family is completely down and out and begging,
then and then only will we talk about help. So we go in a great
deal for remedial services, and frankly we cannot afford this. The
only thing we can afford is something in the way of conservation
and prevention of this deterioration. We don't know all the answers but we know more than we are putting into practice. Family
disorganization doesn't happen like that. It is a process and there
are signs of its happening. The schools know about it, teachers
know about it, and many other people know about it, but nobody
can do anything about it until it gets really bad.

QUESTION: Should our thinking on removing barriers to employment be carried so far that we enact or interpret laws which would

remove all elements of individual preference on the part of the employer? That is, the employer would no longer be allowed to hire one person in preference to another. QUESTION: If you were in a responsible position in a profit-oriented industry where your stockholders expected a reasonable rate of return on their investment, how could you justify the employment of low- or nonproducing individuals regardless of race or sex, or for that matter continue the employment of such individuals already on your payroll?

IRVING KOVARSKY: These questions exhibit that prejudice is universal. I do not advocate a law that would force an employer to take anyone who comes along. I do advocate a law which says that an employer cannot discriminate against a large group simply because their skin is different, they have freckles, perhaps they wear long hair, short pants, or anything of that sort. If you tell me we discriminate against large groups in teaching when we feel they may not have the necessary ability to perform, that is something else. We are not picking at the individual. We may be wrong. We probably are in whom we admit and whom we keep out, but nevertheless, it is not on an individual basis. The second question seems to intimate that as soon as you hire somebody from a minority race, you have an inferior workman. Many of our best athletes today are Negroes simply because they are hungry. This is one way of immediately achieving success. Some of our best entertainers in the world today are Negro. Why would they be less efficient in the factory which does not require as much skill? They are less efficient because the white man has never permitted them to develop efficiency. If this is the case, then it seems that some opportunity must be provided for the Negro to achieve the necessary training in order to operate efficiently. After some training if he is still inefficient (and you will find those just as you would among white people), then by all means throw him out. And you need not worry about the profit picture. Many industries in which you operate are not in competition, they are monopoly type situations. Furthermore, if you provide more income for those who do not have any, they will start buying your products and you will have profit.

QUESTION: Do the individuals in the target audience—those people we are trying to reach on human resources development programs— identify these programs as being relevant to their goals?

JAMES HARRINGTON: My guess would be that they do not identify with these programs as being relevant to their goals, because I question if the programs are designed to be relevant to the goals of the target groups. We do not communicate in many of our programs of health the philosophy which underlines the program but, through the administration of the program, many times we communicate to the target groups that our interest is not so much in helping them as in helping ourselves to "get them off our back" or something like that. Many times in our resource development programs the underlying philosophy through administrative regulations is not that society is truly interested in helping them. By implication, we are communicating to them that the bare minimum is X number of dollars for a mother and three or four children to survive, and we are going to pay them 60 percent of this amount. We are saying, "You're not human, you're two-thirds human." This is why the target group people do not see the programs as being relevant to their own particular goals.

QUESTION: How do we assist the local Negro leaders from being isolated by both the Negro and the white populations?

JAMES THOMAS: You can't assist them in doing this, and furthermore you shouldn't try. One of the problems is the fact that you as the general white population tend to treat Negro leaders as representing all Negroes which in fact in most instances is simply not true. More often than not the local Negro leader is someone who is more closely associated with you as a member of the general population and, therefore, you find him easier to deal with. He is the person to whom you go when anything in the way of a problem comes up, and you discuss it with him as if you were discussing it with all Negroes. This is not the case and we should recognize that. There exists and will continue to exist between Negro leaders and followers a very wide economic gap and also a cultural gap. The problem of "Uncle Tomism" is the greatest problem here, and if once in awhile you are honest with yourself and with these leaders, you will point out to them that they do not have all the answers for the Negro group.

QUESTION: Would you comment on the practicality of moving toward a regional or functional economic level, considering some of the problems you discussed, and also the institutional rigidities that exist out here.

RONALD POWERS: There is a question of whether it is practical to move to regional considerations. Frequently when we talk about regional people, we are talking about more than one state. The practicality of moving to regional development where we involve several states remains to be seen. There are a number of commissions to be formed. There are certain problems in which this seems to be most relevant. For example, we may have water problems if we seriously consider the possibility of putting population in cities that will grow to be not larger than half a million, and consequently have to redirect industry and the like. Regional commissions may be one answer to this in regional development. There are a number of problems with this because states have different laws that sometimes work at cross-purposes. Within any state, if we talk about functional economic areas, what is the practicality of moving to these? Perhaps to try to resolve a number of the structural imbalances. When we think about correcting some institutional imbalances such as the school and the church, area does become a practical device insofar as we get more realistic about how much territory we might have to use to solve a given problem. But one false assumption about areas that may be developing is that there is somehow a one-line world that we can define within space through which all social and economic problems can be solved. There is nothing in economic analysis or sociological analysis that would indicate that we need the same size territory for our schools as we need for mental health centers or other services that relate to human resource development. We need to think of the possibility of educating members of society to have multiple identities with space rather than seeking a one-line world. If we are at the point in this twentieth century that we cannot have a personal identity without a boundary, then we are in deep trouble. We need to think of something larger than most of the jurisdictions in which we operate, because people are mobile over larger areas than the political jurisdictions, but not necessarily for all kinds of service.

QUESTION: Keeping in mind the individual needs and differences, why do many promote the fallacy of always changing the man to fit the social and economic system rather than the process in reverse?

IRVING KOVARSKY: We are not talking about changing the man. We are simply trying to provide an opportunity for the man. There seems to be a notion that somehow, somewhere along the line the Negro isn't the same man as the white person. I would argue with this assumption most strongly. If you go back culturally, you will find that with Columbus and the Portuguese sailors there were Negroes. There is a very high degree of sophistication in the Swahili language. You will find there was a Negro general very important in the Japanese army many years ago. In our type of culture we have sat on the Negro much harder than on any other type known before. When the Romans and the Greeks were functioning in their heyday, slavery existed, but one could buy his way out of slavery. This was typical. In the United States we never permitted that. Where the Portuguese settled in South America, you find a mingling of culture. Nobody looked upon the others as inferior. Yet somehow the attitude has been much harder in the United States than in any other country in the world. The only one that comes close to us today is South Africa, and ours is just more sophisticated.

QUESTION: How would you go about changing our present methods of retiring people from their jobs?

JAMES THOMAS: This is a very difficult problem, and we need to be concerned about it. Many states are developing, along with their experiments in legislation dealing with discrimination on the basis of race and religion, experiments dealing with discrimination based on age. There is no more reason to suspect that our loss is any less or that the problem is any greater in denying a person because of his race or religion than it would be because we arbitrarily say that he is too old to do a job which in fact he can do. One suggestion is to make it a part of our legal structure. Another would be the development of our leisure activities. Leisure is not just something a person is professionally engaged in when he reaches retirement age, but all through our lives today we have leisure programmed in. We need more activities relating to our leisure time in which we can utilize some of our resources. Perhaps our elderly citizens can take a leading part in that development.

QUESTION: In reference to apprenticeship, the entire system is a declining phenomenon partially due to the unrealistically long training period. Thus there exists a need to revamp the entire program. Why are we so interested in a dying system of training?

IRVING KOVARSKY: Apprenticeship is not dying. It is true that many formalized apprentice training programs involving skills have been on the wane, and in some instances the numbers attracted tend to be fewer than those who are retiring. This has been notable in carpentry, brick laying and a number of other skills. Nevertheless, by some definitions of apprentice training, it is on the increase. We have a large number of machines whose operation requires quite a degree of sophistication. Some employers require that their people go to college during the evening in order to develop general sophistication. I consider all of this to be part of the apprentice training effort. Whenever you learn something, when you are a student in class, you are an apprentice.

CHAPTER 10

✸

Needed Directions in
Vocational Resources Development
for the Noncollege Bound

✸

SYLVIA G. McCOLLUM

It is estimated that eight out of ten students now in elementary school will not graduate from college. Cumulatively, this means that during the 1960's alone, 21 million noncollege graduates will enter the labor market. In addition, 3 million wives, mothers, and widows will shift from full-time housework to jobs outside the home during the decade. Add to this the literally millions of already employed workers who need and want additional job-related education and you have a rather clear view of the impressive responsibilities of vocational and technical education in the United States.

RESEARCH AT FEDERAL LEVEL

At the request of President Kennedy in 1961, a panel of consultants named by the Secretary of Health, Education and Welfare studied the whole problem of vocational education in the United States and found what amounted to a critical situation. The panel

Sylvia G. McCollum is Program Planning Officer, Division of Adult and Vocational Research, U.S. Office of Education, Washington, D.C.

was satisfied that the limited number of technical and vocational educational programs which existed at that time were sound but that vocational education offerings were seriously limited—both geographically and in subject matter coverage. None at all was available in many locations. Courses which did exist all too often did not cover areas of training for emerging occupational fields.

In states using federal funds to help support vocational courses in high schools in 1961–62, the Panel of Consultants on Vocational Education found that only a handful of schools was offering training for office and business machine repairmen, medical technicians, and similar training courses designed to prepare workers for employment opportunities outside of traditional vocational education curricula and in fields of rapidly expanding employment opportunities.[1]

The panel made a series of general recommendations to strengthen and extend vocational and technical education. Its report was completed in November, 1962, and was a major contributing factor to the passage of the Vocational Education Act of 1963. This act is concerned with vocational and technical training for *all* occupations requiring less than a baccalaureate degree and for workers of all ages and at all stages of occupational readiness. The reservation of 10 percent of all vocational education appropriations for a research and development program designed to improve vocational education at all levels was another important innovative feature of the act. The federal government's investment in vocational education escalated from some $60 million in 1963–64 to $177 million in 1965–66. The appropriation is scheduled to go up to $225 million in 1966–67 and in each fiscal year thereafter.

These significant changes in federal support of vocational education have been accompanied by equally important changes in federal support of preschool, elementary and secondary, and higher education efforts. I do not think the details of the changes or the dollar amounts of money allocated are as significant as the changes in basic concepts and attitudes, not only at the federal but, more important, at the grass roots, operational level.

A generation ago, American education, for the most part, was structured and operated primarily as an obstacle course which "pushed out" a substantial number of students and permitted only those who could meet clearly defined and frequently inflexible and

---

[1] See "Education for a Changing World of Work," report of the Panel of Consultants on Vocational Education, U.S. Department of Health, Education and Welfare, U.S. Government Printing Office, Washington, D.C., 1963, OE-80021.

irrelevant standards to move on up the line. The vast federal education programs of recent years have begun to shake the foundations of that structure. We are questioning where the failure really lies when we are unable to teach a youngster to read and write and acquire the social and occupational skills necessary to lead a meaningful life. It is not an exaggeration to state that we are well on our way to concluding that, more often than not, the failure *is not* the student's. The very existence of such supplementary education efforts as Head Start, Upward Bound, Job Corps, and others is evidence of that realization.

Another change involves vast reorganizations of curricula. There is growing realization that many areas of study are too narrow and do not provide the student with good education—occupational or otherwise. This development cuts across the total educational spectrum and as a result, we are beginning to see a fusion of general and occupational education. Further, curricula are being revised to increase a student's exposure to subject matter areas beyond his specialized course of study. This development involves a breaking down or at least a closer working relationship between the specialized departments we find in most school systems.[2] We seem to be trying to build bridges between C. P. Snow's "Two Worlds."

Other important changes involve the use of new educational technology, increased and extended "in-service" training of teachers, the introduction of teachers' aides and other subprofessionals into the school system to free the professional educator for professional level work, the rearrangement of physical facilities, increased emphasis on guidance and counseling, and increased vocational and technical offerings in junior colleges throughout the country. These changes reflect a basic upgrading of American education, a commitment of increased resources to education at all levels, and, most important, greater emphasis on the individual student.

The Division of Adult and Vocational Research, which was created to implement the research and development program provided by the Vocational Education Act of 1963, has been deeply involved in the support of projects which reflect these fundamental changes in American education. In fiscal year 1966 our research and demonstration support authorization was $17.75 million. Approximately 550 research, demonstration, and training grant proposals were received from colleges, public or nonprofit agencies, state boards, and local educational institutions seeking financial

---

[2] See for example, "University of Chicago Plans Vast Changes in Curriculum," *Chicago Tribune*, Sep. 20, 1966, as reported in "Daily Press Digest," U.S. Office of Education, Sep. 23, 1966, p. 10.

support. Of these, approximately 200 were approved for funding. In addition, 90 projects started in fiscal 1965 received continuation support during 1966. Grants and/or contracts for research and development projects in vocational education were awarded in 46 states, the District of Columbia, and Puerto Rico. Research is going on in such important areas as curriculum development, the personal and social significance of work, personnel recruitment and development, program organization, administration and evaluation, and occupational information and career choice.

RESEARCH AT STATE LEVEL

In addition, we have supported the creation and operation of 44 State Research Coordinating Units for Vocational Education.[3] These units stimulate and coordinate research and demonstration efforts in vocational education at the local and state level and provide consultative assistance to individuals who wish to prepare research proposals. They also serve as communication links between industry, community agencies, state Labor Departments, state and local offices of the U.S. Employment Service, the U.S. Department of Labor and other sources of manpower information and manpower activity, and vocational education planners and administrators. In a recent speech, Commissioner of Education Harold Howe stated, "If our vocational schools are to fulfill the essential role a technological America expects of them, they must reflect the realities of industrial life. The most important single reality is change. Industry has learned to cope with change as a matter of sheer survival, and it has valuable lessons to pass on to our schools."[4] Two national vocational education research and development centers are also in operation, one at Ohio State University and another at North Carolina State University. The Ohio center has been designated as an Educational Research Information Center (ERIC) clearinghouse and will specialize in vocational education materials. When the Ohio center is fully operational, we will be able to obtain vocational education bibliographies, curriculum materials, guidance and counseling publications, research reports, etc. quickly and efficiently and at a nominal cost.[5]

In addition to support of individual research and demonstra-

---

[3] These units are in operation in all states except Alaska, South Dakota, Maine, Vermont, Maryland, and Virginia.

[4] Harold Howe, "Recruiting for the New Partnership," speech before the Georgia Vocational Association, Atlantic, Mar. 18, 1966.

[5] For additional information regarding ERIC operations see "ERIC" (OE-12022–66), Office of Education, U.S. Department of Health, Education and Welfare, Washington, D.C. 20202.

tion projects and state and national coordinating centers, "4(c)" funds[6] have been used for approximately 60 educational personnel training institutes and workshops involving some 2,400 participants. These institutes were designed to update the skills of vocational education personnel and to provide the opportunity for an interchange among teacher-educators and vocational education leadership at all levels. Eleven seminars have also been held for the development of research competencies of individuals concerned with vocational education research and development activities.

RESEARCH IN THE FUTURE

We anticipate further major research and development efforts in such fields as curriculum development, educational manpower, educational technology, special learning problems—particularly those of the disadvantaged, career development, program evaluation including cost-benefit assessments of alternative educational and training methods, and continued efforts in educational personnel training and development.

Curriculum Development

Vocational education research and development support for new or revised curriculum projects total in excess of $4 million. It has been, and it appears that curriculum revision will continue to be, a major program effort. The Division of Adult and Vocational Research has been assisted in its curriculum development efforts by a special advisory committee comprised of educators, curriculum experts, and representatives of the industrial and labor communities. This committee has identified the essential elements of a good vocational education curriculum. Such a curriculum should:

1. Emphasize the articulation between academic and vocational learning for the purpose of fusing the two programs. Employing vocational preparation as the principal vehicle, the inculcation of basic learning skills could be made more meaningful and relevant to many students who otherwise have difficulty seeing the value of a general education.
2. Expose the student to an understanding of the "real world" through a series of experiences which capitalize on the universal desire of youth to investigate for himself and participate actively in the education process. Abstract, verbal principles would be acquired through nonverbal stimuli, such as seeing, feeling, manipulating, and even smelling.

[6] Vocational Education Act of 1963, P.L. 88–210, Section 4 (c), Dec. 18, 1963, 88th Congress.

3. Train students in both manipulative and cognitive skills, not in just one specialized occupation but in a common core of skills related to a cluster of occupations.

4. Orient students to the attitudes and habits which go with successful performance.

5. Provide a background for the prospective worker by helping him to understand how he fits within the economic and civic institutions of our country.

6. Maximize opportunity for a positive learning experience for students at all levels of abilities and backgrounds.

7. Help students cope with a changing labor market through developing their problem-solving ability and a series of career strategies leading to an adequate level of income and responsibility.

8. Create within the student a sense of self-reliance and awareness which leads him to seek out appropriate careers and aspiration levels.[7]

DAVR, assisted by the Curriculum Development Committee, is considering the desirability of holding a series of regional curriculum development meetings to extend the dialogue on the need for curriculum revision in vocational-technical education.

Such conferences might involve many of the people at the state and local decision-making levels, high schools, post-secondary technical schools, and junior colleges—all who have a vital role to play in occupational curriculum planning and implementation.

Educational and Related Manpower Problems

It appears that increased efforts will be invited to identify emerging occupations and the skills involved in such jobs so that educational planning can reflect the realities of the job market. Attempts to develop appropriate curricula have been accompanied by research directed toward the restructuring of jobs and job relationships in that field of work.[8] The supply and demand picture of educational personnel currently and in the future also needs additional attention. What will the demand for education really be like if all the supplementary education programs such as Head Start, Upward Bound, etc. really succeed? How can we insure a good supply of well-trained, flexible, resourceful teachers and re-

[7] See DAVR internal document titled "DAVR Curriculum Development Advisory Committee," June 12 and 13 Meeting, Washington, D.C.

[8] See "DAVR Research and Development Activities in New Occupational Fields," David S. Bushnell and Sylvia G. McCollum, paper presented at the Twelfth Meeting of the Department of Labor's National Manpower Advisory Committee's Subcommittee on Research, Sep. 23, 1966.

lated supportive personnel? These and similar problems do and will continue to warrant attention in the future.

Educational Technology

Equally significant are the problems surrounding the use of educational technology. Projects are under way which involve and test the use of new computer-based instructional systems, mobile vocational guidance and instructional facilities, and computer-based scheduling of student programs. Any sensible increase of support in this important area presumably would include substantial investments in the evaluation of the new technology. When do these new developments assist in the learning and teaching process and what are their limitations? Under what conditions should they not be used?

Special Learning Problems

We need to improve our understanding of the nonverbal learning process and how it can be used to reach students who lack normal verbal communication skills. We will also be concerned with the nonacademic objectives of education—such as personality, creativity, and social consciousness.

Career Development

What career choices we make seriously affect our basic life styles. We need more research on the internal and external factors which influence these choices. In addition, we need to find ways to increase individual knowledge of the options available to each of us in this important decision-making process.

Program Evaluation

The Vocational Education Act of 1963 requires that a report evaluating federally supported programs in vocational education be presented to the President and Congress not later than January 1, 1968. Research projects designed to contribute to this evaluation are under way. Some are comparative studies of alternative methods of preparing individuals for work including cost-benefit considerations. We envision further substantial investments in this program area as we approach 1968.

CONCLUSION

In the same Georgia speech quoted earlier, Commissioner Howe urged his audience to consider "how the vocational education curriculum can be broadened to develop every student not simply as employee but as citizen, as father or mother, and as a distinctive human person, with a life to live, as well as a living to earn."[9] The Panel of Consultants on Vocational Education in its final report makes the statement: "The best foundation for entering upon a vocational education program is basic general education . . . ."[10] These two statements eloquently describe needed directions for vocational education for the future.

They say, in substance, that we must continue to increase our educational investments until we have established the means to provide each youngster with a solid general and occupational education and each adult with the opportunity for continuing education consistent with his needs and desires.

[9] Howe, *op. cit.*
[10] "Education for a Changing World of Work," *op. cit.*, p. 5.

CHAPTER 11

✳

Needed Directions in Human Resource Development for the College Bound

✳

WILLIAM E. KOENKER

UNDERLYING ALL OF OUR DISCUSSION CONCERNING HUMAN RESOURCE development has been the assumption that the nation should provide challenging educational and employment opportunities to all persons with talent. The objective of enabling every person to have maximum opportunity to achieve the potentiality that lies within him is important in terms of realizing our national goals. These goals include far more than achieving a higher level of Gross National Product. Kenneth Boulding, in a manpower council meeting in 1953, provided a sharp warning that the whole manpower utilization concept was dangerous if it was thought of in terms of increasing physical outputs. Therefore, even though we may use the term "more effective utilization of human resources," we need to keep in mind his injunction that we talk about men in their "infinite variety and sacredness."

WILLIAM E. KOENKER is Vice President for Academic Affairs at the University of North Dakota, Grand Forks, N. Dak., and a member of the Great Plains States Regional Manpower Advisory Committee.

Concern about providing appropriate educational and employment opportunities for youth at all levels of ability is particularly important in the 1960's. This is the decade of the most pronounced population bulge in the adolescent and young adult age group we have ever known. During this decade there will be only a 2.3 percent increase in the age group 25–44, due to the low pre-World War II birth rates; however, for the age category 14–25, there will be a 46 percent increase. This is a rate of increase about three times that which is occurring for the total population. This phenomenal increase in the 14–25 age group reflects the boom in birth rates which started after World War II. This has been responsible for the boom in college enrollments which began early in this decade. The current bulge in the young adult population group makes it important that we be concerned *now* with measures which will make possible the best utilization of all the potential talents and abilities in this group.

This is not a bulge in the college-age population which will end with the current decade and enable us to relax in our concern. Recent census projections of 18- and 19-year-olds indicate a rather regularly rising number until about 1980. This means that we will need to continue to tax our resources and our ingenuity to develop the talent of our youth.

The marked increase in the number of young adults in our population provides at the same time a tremendous resource for national development and an ominous threat of social disaster. If all the potential talents of this younger age group can be developed and given challenging employment, the nation's productive capacity will be enhanced tremendously. Not only can we increase our output of physical goods but we can proceed to enhance the quality of living and remove some of the blights in our present environment. There is, however, an inherent threat in this population bulge if young people do not find challenging opportunities. Not only will their personal ambitions be frustrated, but the cumulative effect of all the individual frustrations can pose a serious threat of social unrest, particularly when it may be heated with racial overtones. There have been times in the past when nations have escaped this problem because a war intervened. Hopefully Viet Nam does not portend this kind of horrible solution to the employment problem of this new generation.

Let us assume that a means short of war will be found to resolve the international problem, and that we can proceed with all possible haste with a program which will make constructive use of the available talents of all our young people. What are the essential aspects of such a program? What are the needed directions for this resource development and utilization? The most critical, overriding factor in the solution is to achieve and sustain a high level of economic activity. If this can be realized, then all other things are possible—we can have the tax resources to divert into educational programs, and we can supply the job opportunities necessary. But a high and sustained level of economic activity will not result from the fortuitous merging of economic forces in a free market. Most rational economists have long since been disabused of that notion. A high level of economic activity will be sustained only if Congress and the administrative branches of the government will use the best mixture of monetary, fiscal, and debt management policy at their disposal.

It is significant, however, that one of the critical barriers to achieving a high level of economic activity may be the shortage of scientific and technically trained manpower. If we attain a high level of employment, it is expected that total employment by 1975 will increase by about 23 percent; however, we will need an increase in professional, scientific, and technical workers of about 48.6 percent. The number of workers in this category will need to increase from 8.9 to about 13.2 million. This means that we will have in this professional classification almost as many workers as we will have in the service category.

Let us focus attention on what can be done to develop the talent of the college bound. Some of the experts discussing the problem argue that if we maintain our current programs for aiding capable students to proceed through college, we can meet the overall needs for professional, scientific, and technical personnel. However, even if we achieve the overall goal, there are still likely to be serious gaps in certain specific employment catgories. One of the specific areas in which a shortage is expected is engineering. It is expected that the supply of new graduates plus those transferring in from other fields plus persons without degrees being upgraded will amount to only about 450,000 in the 1960's. In contrast, the demand will amount to about 700,000. This imbalance, particularly for electrical and mechanical engineers, will require that we attract more students into engineering programs, that we reduce attrition in these schools, and that we improve the utilization of engineering graduates.

Another area in which there has been a shortage is the area of college teachers. It is generally agreed that there will still be a shortage of properly qualified college teachers (those with the doctorate) for the next few years. There is, however, a considerable difference of opinion about what the supply-demand situation is going to be beyond 1970. Until very recently it was believed that there would be a marked shortage all the way to the 1980's. However, some errors have been found in the Office of Education projections. The current production of 16,500 Ph.D.'s annually is twice what the Office of Education projected ten years ago. A very recent projection by Allan Cartter for the American Council on Education indicates that by 1980 the supply of new doctorates will increase from the present 16,500 to 55,000 annually. He estimates that there will be 20,000 new doctorates available for teaching by 1980 and only 10,000 needed to preserve the present ratio of 50 percent doctorate degree holders among faculty members of four-year colleges. There are minor variations between fields in the longer-term supply-demand situation, but generally Cartter predicts an excess supply in most college teaching fields. The marked contrast between this recent analysis showing a surplus of college teachers and the earlier warnings about shortages indicates the perils of forecasting in the manpower area, but also reveals the need for more reliable estimates of supply and demand.

A significant aspect of college teaching and all other professional and scientific fields is that more and more post-baccalaureate education is being required. The amount of time which must elapse between decisions to enter these fields and employment availability makes the adjustment of supply and demand a rather precarious business. Because of the long training period required, it is important that we develop better ways of forecasting demand and then take the necessary steps to encourage people to enter fields where shortages will occur. Thus far we have been depending on the forces of the market—the shortages known to exist in some fields, the redundancies in others—to bring about an equilibrium position. The market does this, but after much lag, many frustrated career expectations, and unfilled positions. Predicting occupational requirements ten years hence is difficult, but the new *Occupational Outlook Handbook* is evidence that progress can be and is being made. With better forecasting, colleges and high schools can do a more adequate job of advising students and structuring their own programs to meet the shortages.

In addition to better forecasting of demand, we need better organization of the market for professional and scientific manpower. The state employment service seems to be reasonably effective for industrial and clerical workers in the local areas, but the present clearance system for interstate placements is hopelessly slow and antiquated. The College Placement Council, with its new computerized system, has promise of doing an excellent job for the current college graduates. However, for experienced job seekers in most scientific and professional fields, there is a most haphazard approach to matching job seekers and jobs. There is urgent need for the employment service to get on with development of a national system for placement which will be less protective of local labor markets. This is one of the most obvious steps which could be taken to enhance labor mobility, especially for professional and scientific people.

Improved forecasting of demand and facilitating mobility will not, however, provide the increased supply of professional, scientific, and technical people we need in many fields. It will not seek out the people with talent and provide the encouragement and educational opportunities needed. To accomplish this innovation and development, some new directions are called for.

There is needed, first of all, better identification of talent by at least the junior high school level. Identification is needed this early if talented youngsters are to be given high school programs which genuinely challenge their capabilities. The potential mathematician, engineer, or scientist needs to be identified by the ninth grade, if he is to be given anything more than the puerile pap fed to most high school students today. If he gets nothing more than this, he will not be able to handle college programs in the professional and scientific areas and his exceptional talents are likely to be permanently wasted. The redeeming aspect of the universal secondary school system in the United States is that most schools have developed a differentiated track system so that the college bound can be given an adequate foundation.

One of the ways to identify talent is through nationally designed standard tests. These are now more likely, however, to be given to students in the senior year rather than in junior high. We need something like the National Merit Tests, the Scholastic Aptitude Tests, or the American College Tests to identify talent—or at least the critically important verbal ability—at an earlier stage. Apprehension about mass testing is currently being expressed, but there is not much rationality in it. The concern seems to come mainly from those people who have an instinctive dislike for persons with superior ability and would prefer that they not be drawn out from the undifferentiated mass.

There is need, however, to develop tests in which results are less influenced by environment and past training. We need tests which more fully reflect the innate capacities of many individuals from economically, socially, or culturally deprived backgrounds. We also need tests which will better identify creative and imaginative ability, so that more gifted people in the arts and elsewhere can be given the kind of opportunity they deserve.

In conjunction with better identification of talent, there needs to be better educational counseling in the high schools. With the marked trend toward an increasing proportion of students attending college, there is less need for job counseling and more need for orienting students to the whole realm of post-high school educational opportunities. Students need help in achieving a realistic assessment of their own capabilities and then in selecting the college and the curriculum which are most appropriate.

Despite the marked increase in the proportion of high school graduates who attend college, there is still a substantial amount of unused college potential. In a recent paper Daniel P. Moynihan, former Assistant Secretary of Labor, estimated that about 50 percent of the population had the ability to achieve a score of 100 on the General Aptitude Test used by the United States Employment Service and that this was the score necessary to do acceptable junior college work. However, only 23 percent of the population have completed one to three years of college. Those who have the capability for completing four years of college constitute about 31 percent of the population, but only 11 percent of the population have actually completed this much college work. The people who have the abilities to do acceptable postgraduate college work constitute, according to his estimates, about 16 percent of the population; however, it is significant that only about 4 percent, or less than one-fourth of these, actually completed a year or more of graduate work. For women, the disparity is even greater—only one-tenth of the women who had the capability of doing graduate work have finished a year or more of graduate study. Stating this in terms of numbers, Moynihan estimated that in one year (1960) there were about 240,000 young men and 345,000 young women who had the ability to achieve a college education but who failed to attend college. These data indicate there there is need for programs like Project Talent and Upward Bound to search out talented but culturally deprived youngsters, and to provide financial assistance where appropriate.

There is, fortunately, a rather clear tendency for students in the higher ability groupings to attend college. They are less likely to be discouraged by the prospect of failure, and they are more aware of the personal and economic gains. In the study *Project Talent,* it was found that of the students who attended college, 70 percent had scores above the 60th percentile rank. Of the group

who did not attend college, only 28 percent had scores above this
range. These data indicate, however, that as more and more students are given an opportunity to attend college, these new college
students will include a larger proportion of students in the middle
range ability group. Many of these students would have the ability
to complete a junior college program but not a four-year degree
program.

With this tendency to draw more students from the middle
range of ability, colleges will need to adapt their programs to this
new reality. The most significant aspect of that adaptation is the
development of the community colleges with responsibility for
providing vocational education programs for the local community
and providing two years of transfer credit courses. One of the
critical needs in higher education is for more diversity in institutions. Institutions need to become more specialized in the programs
they offer, and to select students accordingly. Instead of developing
programs to fit the needs of the special group of students they set
out to serve, junior colleges strive to be more like four-year colleges, and state colleges are all trying to become universities. It
seems that neither the accrediting agencies nor the new state coordinating boards are able to do much about this. Like the automobile makers of the last decade, the colleges are unwilling to offer
a truly differentiated product, and the result is that students with
widely varying interests and abilities do not have an adequate range
of choice.

Most colleges are also quite reluctant to alter the lockstep type
of curriculum in which whole classes move through similar programs at the same pace. From a comptroller's point of view, this is
fine for cutting unit costs, but it is terribly frustrating to students
whose abilities and interests differ substantially from the mode.
Fortunately, the better schools are accepting the principle of advanced placement, independent study, and honors programs to
challenge those students who have exceptional ability.

Even if all colleges had the most enlightened leadership, they
lack the resources to establish programs which will adequately
match opportunities with talent. The states lack the resources to
cope with the continuing rise in enrollments. Private colleges are
finding their endowments more and more inadequate and are
therefore forced to charge higher tuition fees. It seems only reasonable that since the federal government, directly or indirectly, is
the largest consumer of professional and technically trained manpower, they have a responsibilty to help educate them. It is es-

timated that about 120,000 scientific and technically trained people
are now directly employed by the federal government, and another
300,000 are working on government-financed programs in industry.
The federal government's share of the total research and development budget was less than 20 percent prior to World War II. Currently it is estimated to comprise about two-thirds of the total.

The only time that the federal government made an adequate
contribution to higher education was during the period of the
G.I. bill. During the first two or three years after World War II,
federal expenditures on higher education were more than half of
all public expenditures on post-secondary education. The readiness
of young men to take advantage of collge is indicated by the fact
that 60 percent of those under 25 made use of this G.I. bill eligibility. Since the early 1950's, however, the vast increase in expenditure on education has been borne by the states. This burden has
more than quadrupled during the past 15 years. In 1948 federal
expenditures on education amounted to 38 percent of total public
expenditures for education. This dropped to 30 percent in 1950,
but then dropped rapidly to 8 percent in 1954 and 5 percent in
1963. With the Elementary and Secondary Education Act, the
Higher Education Facilities Act, and the Higher Education Act,
there has been a signicant increase in the federal share. However,
this new level will need to be at least sustained if not increased if
we are going to provide decent opportunities to the increasing
number of capable young people who want a college education.

The states vary markedly in the effort they make to support
higher education. This variation is particularly evident in data
indicating dollars spent for operating expenses for higher education relative to personal income available. Some states are making
a very substantial effort—for example, Utah is spending $13.57 for
higher education per $1,000 of personal income; Wyoming $10.97;
and Colorado, $9.60. At the other extreme, there are states like
Massachusetts which spends only $1.83. It is significant, however,
that the states which are making the most sincere effort are frequently not the states that are best able to compete for the products
of their own educational system.

The market for engineers, scientists, and college professors is
a national market, and most recruiting is done on a national scale.
The states which tax more heavily to produce a large supply of
baccalaureate and graduate degree candidates are very frequently
the states with lower wage rates. Hence other states or regions may
"compete away" their products. The national competition for pro-

fessional and scientific manpower points up again the need to channel federal funds to the schools and the states that are making the principal efforts to provide an adequate supply.

The effort to meet the demands for scientific and technical manpower must be a national effort. Many states do not find it in their self-interest to make the effort which is necessary. Those states which are willing to make a substantial effort do not have financial resources commensurate with the numbers which they have to educate. The Educational Facilities Act and the Higher Education Act indicate that we are beginning to recognize the national interest and obligation for improved higher education. As we continue to fuse federal support into our system of state-financed and privately financed colleges and universities, we will need to make sure that the dollars will go where the students are and where the best programs exist. We will also need better forecasts of manpower needs, and then a system for getting this information to students early enough so that they can properly plan their college careers. We also need to exert pressure on the colleges and the state coordinating commissions to provide the diverse educational opportunities needed to provide a challenge to the whole spectrum of youth potential.

However, after we identify talent of all kinds and provide better counseling services and easier access to educational opportunity, we may still fall short of reaching our goal. We need, finally, to pursue the kind of economic policies, in both the public and the private sector, which will insure adequate and appropriate job opportunities. The frustration of young people who have achieved a sound education but are unable to find reasonably challenging jobs may be worse than the frustration of having been denied educational opportunities in the first place.

✳

Evaluation
of Manpower Development Programs

✳

GERALD G. SOMERS

THE DEFINITION OF CONCEPTS IS A SERIOUS CONCERN WHEN WE TALK about an evaluation of human resource development, and some clarification is needed. There is a difference between policies to develop human beings and policies to develop human resources and policies to develop manpower. A program to improve the status of human beings includes not only education and training in labor market activities but health and environmental factors, including air pollution, water pollution, and the concerns of all the social sciences. When we talk about human resources, we are talking about an economic concept. A resource in economics is a factor of production, and human resources represent the human factors in production. This notion of human development that contributed to economic production is narrower than the total development of human beings. "Manpower" is even narrower than that, although it comes fairly close to this concept of human resources. Manpower development includes policies that increase the worker's

---

GERALD G. SOMERS is Professor of Economics and Director of the Industrial Relations Research Institute, University of Wisconsin, Madison, Wis.

productivity or increase his mobility so that he makes a greater productive contribution in the labor market and at the same time increases his own earnings and welfare.

MANPOWER RETRAINING AND RELOCATION

This chapter focuses on two particular manpower development policies rather than on the whole gamut of human resource development policies. Even in these two areas, retraining and relocation, evaluation is difficult and little has been attempted. If we go beyond these two specific policies, we run into even more imponderables and find even less research evaluation. What of new vocational education programs, Operation Head Start, or some of the remedial education programs? We do not know how these are paying off.

Retraining

An evaluation of retraining is important simply because so much of the federal money in the manpower field is going into retraining; and it cuts across so much of the legislation passed in the last few years. There has been a revolution in this field. Since 1961–62, with the passing of the Area Redevelopment Act and the Manpower Development and Training Act, the federal government for the first time has undertaken on a vast scale to retrain the unemployed and the underemployed in order to raise their income and their employment opportunities. The poverty program is definitely focused on retraining and is included in the Trade Expansion Act; and if we add the Vocational Education Act of 1963, which also stressed training programs for the disadvantaged as well as improvements in general vocational education, we have a complete picture of a revolutionary development in so-called creative federalism.

And yet with all the hundreds of millions of dollars that have gone into these programs and the amendments and the continued amendments and the support they have received from Congress, we are not sure as to the benefits and costs of MDTA programs relative to alternative policies. We do not know whether the funds spent on these programs are more wisely spent than they would be in simply giving income payments to the unemployed and the disadvantaged. The funds could be spent on labor mobility projects to try to move workers to jobs or to increase their job information or simply to educate them. There is a variety of expenditures on human resources that might conceivably pay off better than retraining programs, so it is important to evaluate them.

Relocation

The second area topic to be discussed is the program to increase the mobility of labor. These two approaches are at the heart of manpower policy—increasing skills and increasing mobility. We hope to move workers from areas of labor surplus where there are no jobs to areas of labor demand. The policy involves increasing the information which will permit workers to know where the jobs are in distant localities and then giving them the wherewithal to reach those jobs. This program is important not because we spend very much money on it at the moment but because we are now just beginning to experiment with it. Demonstration relocation projects are under way throughout the country. It is very important to evaluate them because we are likely to expand these projects into a permanent program, again without fully knowing whether they are more beneficial than alternative policies.

Even if we were to accept the basic notion on faith that retraining and increased mobility of labor are generally sound social investments, we would still wish to make concrete, research evaluations of particular kinds of MDTA programs. Should we put more money into the training of women as nurses aides or into the training of men as machinists? Should we subsidize employers so that they will undertake on-the-job training programs or subsidize vocational education to train workers institutionally? These are very important questions because the halcyon days are over in the human resource development and manpower fields. Congress is no longer as generous as it was. A few years ago almost anything proposed in the field of human resource development went sailing through Congress. The manner in which the MDTA program was amended, improved, and expanded in 1963 and in 1965 without any conclusive demonstration of its payoff is an indication that in those days it took very little to convince Congressmen that such measures were worthwhile. But now we are cutting back on these expenditures. The antipoverty program is in trouble, MDTA is in trouble. We finally come down to the classic economic problem—the allocation of scarce resources. We must look at the costs and benefits of alternative programs not only in economic terms but in social and psychological terms. And we should try to insure that when we invest scarce dollar resources in one kind of training, it is at least as sound an investment in human beings as other kinds of training or other manpower policies.

We just do not have the answers. Let us look at the MDTA, for instance. What do we know about its results? We are told that over 70 percent of the trainees have been placed on jobs. If we accept this figure at face value, it appears to be a notable accomplishment because presumably all of these people, or almost all of them, were unemployed prior to their training. But does this placement ratio really tell us very much about the accomplishments of MDTA training? The crucial question for every government-sponsored human resource development program is what would be the situation in the absence of that program? Here we have to ask this crucial question, "What would be the case in the absence of the MDTA?"

In the present stage of our economy, with the unemployment rate that has steadily moved below 4 percent, it is likely that most of the MDTA trainees would have obtained jobs even if they had not taken training, and even though they had some record of unemployment prior to the MDTA course. This is a reasonable assumption because characteristics of regular MDTA trainees reveal that most are the "cream of the crop" of the unemployed. Their educational level is higher and their age is lower than the average of the unemployed in the areas from which they are drawn.

One cannot blame the officials in the employment service for this selectivity. They are charged with this procedure in the legislation itself. The MDTA says that regular trainees should have a reasonable expectation of employment. Thus, there is little point in selecting a worker with less than an eighth grade education, over 60 years of age, who has no recent employment, and try to place him on a job after a few months in an accelerated training course.

How can we tell what would have happened in the absence of training? The best way of finding out is to have a control group of people who are similar to the trainees in every characteristic with the exception of not having had training. For example, take a male Negro who is 50 years of age, has an eighth grade education, has had two years of unemployment just prior to his training, and follow up on him three years after his training course as a machine operator. Then take another worker with the same sex, race, age, education, and previous unemployment—who did not have the training—and see what happens to him after the same period of time. You may find that the trainee obtained a job and increased his earnings and the nontrainee got no job or one at a much lower level of earnings. If we had a large enough probability sample of trainees and nontrainees we might be convinced that the training pays off.

Unfortunately we can seldom get this kind of controlled experiment. The government agencies reporting on retraining have made little attempt at such research. In some of our own studies we have tried to establish such control groups. For instance, in West Virginia, and to a smaller extent in Tennessee and a few other places, we selected people who were unemployed at the same time as the trainees, and we compared their experience after the training period with the trainees. But the trouble with these private efforts is that samples are necessarily very small and one can never be certain about the generalization that is drawn from such studies. Nonetheless, much more of this sort of study should be made.

Evaluation of Training Programs for the Disadvantaged

A similar approach is required to evaluate programs for retraining the disadvantaged. If we say that regular MDTA courses are taking the cream of the crop, people who might have obtained jobs anyway, we then have to ask what would happen if they chose more of the hard core of the disadvantaged.

There have been even fewer evaluations of retraining programs for the disadvantaged. In Milwaukee we looked at training programs for public welfare recipients and we matched trainees with other welfare recipients who were not trained on the basis of six or seven common characteristics. But here again, we had a very small sample, leading to only tentative conclusions.

These studies show that we have to be very clear in defining the benefits of the investment in training and manpower policies for the disadvantaged. If we compare public welfare recipients with trainees drawn from the less hard-core unemployed, whites and better educated, etc., we find that disadvantaged trainees do badly: they do not get jobs as readily, their employment rate is down to 40 or 35 percent, and their post-training earnings are not nearly as high as those of the more advantaged groups graduating from MDTA programs. Are we then to conclude on the basis of a hard, cold, benefit-cost analysis that this is a bad investment? We should not, because if we take an entirely different approach, it turns out to be a very good investment. If we compare the results in employment and earnings of the disadvantaged trainee with the disadvantaged nontrainee, we find a bigger gap than between other trainees and nontrainees. If the control group is a similar group of hard-core unemployed welfare recipients who did not receive training, we find that training pays off very well.

The same is true of older trainees. We have to face the fact that older trainees do not do as well as younger trainees who are otherwise similarly situated, who have the same education, for instance, and the same pretraining histories in the labor market. It is a mistake to contend that training an older worker necessarily makes him the equal of a younger worker with the same kind of training. But it is true that an older trainee does much better than an older nontrainee with the same level of education and other similar characteristics; and in that sense, it is a very good investment. The payoff in earnings and employment opportunity exceeds the economic cost.

This discussion of benefits and costs excludes the socio-psychological measurements. They are harder to evaluate than the dollars and cents of earnings, though psychologists and sociologists tell us that there are measures that could be employed to test the values of training programs in these terms.

LABOR MOBILITY PROGRAM

Turning from evaluation of training, let us consider briefly the mobility program. Here we find even greater difficulties. Looking at the results for individuals, does relocation enhance a man's employment and earnings? There are a number of pilot relocation projects under the MDTA with the expectation that they will later be adopted on a national scale. It is likely that when funds become more readily available, subsidized relocation will become a major part of our so-called "active manpower policy."

For some years now European countries have paid workers to move from depressed economic areas to areas of labor demand. Whether one thinks that the unemployment of recent years was caused by increasing structural problems or deficient aggregate demand, there is no doubt that there are serious structural problems. Part of the sructural problem is that we have areas like Appalachia, where there is a surplus of labor, and we have other areas like Milwaukee, where there is a tight labor shortage. In Milwaukee there are fewer than 2 percent unemployed, whereas in West Virginia communities there are still 15 to 20 percent unemployed. When labor shortages are developing and when inflationary pressures are increasing because of those labor shortages, surely it makes sense to move workers from depressed areas to the areas of labor demand. In fact, some will say if you did that, you would not need all these training programs. There are said to be many workers in depressed areas who have at least enough skill to fill the semiskilled jobs in Milwaukee for which training courses have been established.

This points to the need for a careful evaluation. Here we have two manpower programs, both run by the same agency of government, that might very well conflict with each other. For example, they are moving workers into Milwaukee from northern Michigan and northern Wisconsin. Those are traditionally somewhat depressed areas. There has never been a sufficient economic base to employ the population of that northern tier of counties across Michigan, Wisconsin, and Minnesota. The iron mining has died out, the timber industry is dying out, and few expanding industries have taken their place. And yet Milwaukee, not very many miles away, is booming. And the government is subsidizing the movement of workers into Milwaukee. There are two questions that have to be raised in evaluating that kind of program: What does it do for the workers themselves, and what does it do for the region and the economy?

There seems to be considerable evidence that the economic position of the mobile workers is enhanced. However, there are social and psychological costs in moving. The mobile workers miss their friends and the familiar surroundings of their home town, but in most cases they make a rational calculation—rational in economic terms—to stay in the area of higher earnings and greater employment opportunities. Even though many studies seem to indicate an improvement in earnings, without a carefully selected control group of nonmobile workers in the home area, we still cannot be sure of this improvement in a period such as the present. We do know that in northern Michigan and northern Wisconsin employment conditions have greatly improved. They were "depressed areas" when the relocation projects were first authorized a year or so ago, but they have been officially removed from the depressed area category and most of the workers there now have jobs. Perhaps their earnings are not as high as earnings in Milwaukee, but they do have jobs.

Let us assume, even though we do not have definitive proof, that the mobility pays off. It is a reasonable assumption, since the cost of the government's relocation program is not great (maybe $200 on the average), and the return seems to be considerable in higher earnings, even though there may be a socio-psychological cost. But what about the area they left and the area to which they go? The Chamber of Commerce in the area they left in northern Michigan might have some real questions in its evaluation of this program. Spokesmen from some depressed areas have complained to Congress that they "are suffering loss of population anyway and along comes the government paying more of their population to move." In many cases they have already lost the cream of their labor force, the younger people; and most of the people the government is moving also tend to be the "best" of that labor force. Relatively young workers are the only ones who really want to move even under the incentive of government aid. Older, less skilled people do not want to move, and even the incentive of government transportation allowances does not seem to be enough.

And so the Chamber of Commerce that sees the empty stores, the clergymen who see the empty churches, point to the real economic loss, the lost investment in physical capital. There have been schools and churches as well as stores built in this area, and these are in danger of going to waste as the work force departs.

Another very serious question in evaluating this kind of program concerns the people in Milwaukee. What about those hardcore unemployed Negroes who are still unemployed in the central section of Milwaukee even though there is a 2 percent unemployment rate and generally a tight labor market? We still have thousands of unemployed people in this category even in Milwaukee. Employers have been bypassing those people. They could readily bypass them in the earlier years of this decade because of the surplus of labor in Milwaukee. There has been enough unemployment so that employers could raise their standards of hiring enough to completely exclude Negro unemployed workers with low levels of skill and education.

Now we are moving toward the point in Milwaukee where the labor market is tight enough so that Milwaukee employers may be forced to hire these hard-core unemployed Negroes. But instead of that, some of them are now able to hire "white Anglo-Saxon Protestants" from northern Michigan and northern Wisconsin, and they much prefer them, especially since many of the workers coming from northern Michigan have taken some training in the Marquette training center. Beyond that they consider them much more pliable, and also the element of discrimination enters here. So we have a situation where government programs presumably designed to reduce unemployment may be aggravating the unemployment situation of certain people in Milwaukee, and the same thing is happening in other cities.

NEED FOR EVALUATION OF PROGRAMS

We need to be somewhat more hardheaded in our evaluation of all of these human resource development programs. This is not to say that, given a hardheaded evaluation, we will then conclude that the programs were wrong, that we should not have conducted them, that we should not pass more legislation along this line, because basically these policies are probably fruitful. But we have to persuade people in Congress that we have made such an evaluation, that they are not buying a "pig in a poke." Congressmen and others are starting to ask pressing, embarrassing questions. "How do you know this is good?" "How do you know this kind of program is better than that kind of program?" "How do you know a combination of training and relocation is a good thing in a particular area?" "How do you know that they are not conflicting with each other?" "What is the best way of integrating the two?"

These are serious questions even if we restrict our inquiry to the level of the individual and of a particular city or region. When we ask the other question, "What is the impact on the economy as a whole?" we almost have to throw up our hands in complete despair. We do not really know whether the MDTA training program has reduced total unemployment nationally by one little bit. Some say it has had little impact along this line. Yet Congress passed the MDTA as an attack against unemployment in a period when unemployment rates were 6 and 7 percent. To answer the query, "Has the MDTA training program reduced total unemployment?" you have to have raised such basic questions as "What happens to those people who did not get the retraining?" We know that MDTA training has just been a drop in the bucket. We have had a few hundred thousand trainees out of the millions who are still unemployed, even at the 4 percent level. We have taken only a small segment of the unemployed from the labor market and trained them; 70 percent of them got jobs, and their earnings went up, but does this not place those unemployed people who did not get training at an even greater disadvantage? Have we simply changed the order in the line that queues outside the unemployment compensation office? Until we can answer the question as to whether trainees merely displace nontrainees in the employed job market, we cannot be sure of the impact of the training program on national employment levels. If we could say that training had *created* any jobs or *increased mobility* toward jobs, we could feel a little more certain and say it must be helping the national unemployment picture; but we have no sure proof of that either. Some contend that training merely gives a worker the capability of taking a job that is open. It seldom creates one for him. One way the MDTA training programs may create jobs is that if the government is spending so much money on training, they are then expanding total demand, and this expansion of total demand is raising the GNP and the demand for labor. But retraining still is on a small scale, and I doubt if it has had much impact on the expansion of demand as yet.

TRAINING AND INFLATION

On the other side of the coin many people are now saying that the real value of the training and relocation programs is not to reduce unemployment; the real purpose is to combat inflation. Manpower programs are finally coming into their own. Now that we have inflation, this is the time to expand these programs. We have shortages of labor; we have unemployed people, and by all means let us train them, let us move them so that they fill those job shortages, and thereby reduce the inflationary pressure. Unfortunately we have no proof that this is happening either, and it would be difficult to establish that this has taken place.

Since manpower programs are on a small scale at the present time, the presumption is they have not done much to combat inflationary pressures. Hopefully, if we expanded these programs greatly, they might satisfy some of the inflationary demand. But there is one thing we must bear in mind when we say the training really comes into its own in an inflationary period. Not only do the potential benefits go up, since we are more likely to be able to place a trainee on a job in a period of full employment, but the costs also go up in this period, and a cost-benefit calculation should be made to see whether training really pays off more in such a period compared with a period of unemployment. What are these increased costs? The costs essentially are the shortages of the training instructors. In such a period as the present there is a great shortage of people qualified to conduct training courses, and the tighter the full employment, the greater the shortage. Every time we use somebody to train workers in a period of full employment, we are taking him off some other worthy pursuit. We want to be sure that what we are taking him off is not more important than the new program. Another cost element that goes up in such a period is the opportunity cost of the trainee himself—a term we use in economics meaning what he might have been doing if he had not been taking training. Most of the trainees in such a period as the present with relatively full employment could be working during the time they are in training. But if they are taking training, they do not have this opportunity. That cost goes up in a period of full employment. In a period of depression they might be unemployed anyway and thus would not be contributing to production during their period of training.

These are just a few of the problems of evaluation, and these two examples are worth stressing as tests of evaluation methodology. We could apply the same kinds of arguments to almost every other piece of human resource development legislation. In fact, many others are even tougher to determine. My plea for evaluation is that we simply ought to know what we are doing, and we ought to be able to choose intelligently between a variety of alternatives. We ought to be able to confront the critics of these programs with some fairly hard data—at least convince them that we have tried to evaluate manpower policies.

✴

Program of Conference
on Human Resources Development
October 13–14, 1966, Iowa State University
Ames, Iowa

✴

FIRST SESSION

Concepts and Problems of Human Resources Development
Welcome Address, *Marvin A. Anderson*
Chairman, *Lee Kolmer*
Keynote Address, "The Concept and Problems of Human Resources Development," *Harold L. Sheppard*
Discussants, *J. Earl Williams,* "The Economist and Human Resource Development"; *Austin E. Miller, S.J.,* "Social Justice and Human Resource Development"

SECOND SESSION

Need and Demand for Human Resources Development
A. THE NATIONAL PICTURE
Chairman, *Harold W. Davey*
Speaker, *Kenneth E. Boulding,* "Human Resources Development as a Learning Process"
Speaker, *Edgar Weinberg,* "Service Sector Employment Trends"

THIRD SESSION

Need and Demand for Human Resources Development
B. THE IOWA SCENE
Chairman, *C. Phillip Baumel*
Speaker, *Eber Eldridge*, "Agricultural Employment Trends"
Speaker, *Gene Futrell*, "Manufacturing Employment Trends"

FOURTH SESSION

Banquet
Chairman, *Edward B. Jakubauskas*
Speaker, *Joseph G. Colmen*, "Is Horatio Alger Dead?"

FIFTH SESSION

Barriers to Human Resources Development
Chairman, *George M. Beal*
Speaker, *Irving Kovarsky*, "Racial Barriers in Apprentice Training
    Programs"
Discussants, *James W. Harrington*, "Physical and Mental Barriers";
    James A. Thomas, "Institutional Barriers"; *Ronald C. Powers*,
    "Social and Spatial Barriers"

SIXTH SESSION

Needed Directions in Human Resources Development
Chairman, *Julia M. Faltinson*
Speaker, *Sylvia G. McCollum*, "Needed Directions in Vocational
    Resources Development for the Noncollege Bound"
Speaker, *William E. Koenker*, "Needed Directions in Human Re-
    source Development for the College Bound"
Speaker, *Gerald G. Somers*, "Evaluation of Manpower Development
    Programs"

✳

Conference Contributors

✳

MARVIN A. ANDERSON: Dean, University Extension Service, Iowa State University, Ames, Iowa.

C. PHILLIP BAUMEL: Associate Professor of Economics, Iowa State University, Ames, Iowa.

GEORGE M. BEAL: Professor of Sociology, Iowa State University, Ames, Iowa.

KENNETH E. BOULDING: Professor of Economics, University of Michigan, Ann Arbor, Mich. President-elect, American Economics Association.

JOSEPH G. COLMEN: Deputy Assistant Secretary for Education, U.S. Department of Health, Education and Welfare, Washington, D.C.

HAROLD W. DAVEY: Chairman, Industrial Relations Advisory Committee and Professor of Economics, Iowa State University, Ames, Iowa.

EBER ELDRIDGE: Professor of Economics, Iowa State University, Ames, Iowa.

JULIA M. FALTINSON: Associate Dean, College of Home Economics, Iowa State University, Ames, Iowa. Member, Great Plains States Regional Manpower Advisory Committee.

GENE A. FUTRELL: Associate Professor of Economics, Iowa State University, Ames, Iowa.

JAMES A. HARRINGTON: Member, Board of Control of State Institutions, State of Iowa, Des Moines, Iowa.

EDWARD B. JAKUBAUSKAS: Professor of Economics, Iowa State University, Ames, Iowa. Director of the Industrial Relations Center at Iowa State University. Formerly Director of the Iowa State Manpower Development Council.

WILLIAM E. KOENKER: Vice President for Academic Affairs, University of North Dakota, Grand Forks, N. Dak. Member, Great Plains States Regional Manpower Advisory Committee.

LEE KOLMER: State Leader, Agricultural and Economic Development, Cooperative Extension Service, Iowa State University, Ames, Iowa.

IRVING KOVARSKY: Professor of Industrial Relations of Law, University of Iowa, Iowa City, Iowa.

SYLVIA G. McCOLLUM: Program Planning Officer, Division of Adult and Vocational Research, U.S. Office of Education, Washington, D.C.

AUSTIN E. MILLER, S.J.: Chairman, Social Order Conference, Creighton University, Omaha, Neb. Chairman, Great Plains States Regional Manpower Advisory Committee.

RONALD C. POWERS: Associate Professor of Sociology, Iowa State University, Ames, Iowa.

HAROLD L. SHEPPARD: Staff Social Scientist, W. E. Upjohn Institute of Employment Research, Washington, D.C.

JAMES A. SOCKNAT: Deputy Director, Iowa State Manpower Development Council, Des Moines, Iowa. Member, Iowa Bar Association.

GERALD G. SOMERS: Professor of Economics and Director, Industrial Relations Research Institute, University of Wisconsin, Madison, Wis.

JAMES A. THOMAS: Executive Director, Iowa Civil Rights Commission, Des Moines, Iowa.

EDGAR WEINBERG: Chief, Division of Technological Studies, U.S. Bureau of Labor Statistics, Washington, D.C.

J. EARL WILLIAMS: Professor of Economics and Director, Human Resources Institute, University of Houston, Houston, Tex.

Index